Anna MANCINI

Ancient Roman Solutions to Modern Legal Issues

The Example of Patent Law

Buenos Books America
www.buenosbooks.us

Hardcover 2d edition 2007
ISBN : 978-1-932848-35-9

PUBLISHED BY BUENOS BOOKS AMERICA
http://www.buenosbooks.us
Info@buenosbooks.us
Other editions available :
PAPERBACK: ISBN 978-1-932848-36-6
E-BOOK 1st edition: ISBN 1-932848-05-3

French version published by Buenos Books
International (www.BuenosBooks.fr)
Title : Les solutions de l'ancien droit romain
aux problèmes juridiques modernes

CAUTION: Please do not photocopy this book. Buy
the electronic version instead: cheap, convenient and meets
the author's rights.
E-books available on our Websites:
http://www.buenosbooks.us
(in French) http://www.buenosbooks.fr

CONTENTS

iv

PREFACE

Although the origin of ancient Roman law is lost in the mists of time, this law is still alive. With the expansion of the Roman Empire, this ancient legal knowledge was carried in both the western and the eastern worlds. After the fall of the Roman Empire in 476 A.D., the Roman legal system progressively faded away. Then a rebirth took place in the 12th Century when ancient Roman law was taken as a model to shape European legal systems. Consequently modern legal systems owe a great deal to ancient Roman law and still bear its imprint, mainly in their foundation, their structure and in the legal vocabulary. Ancient Roman law concepts are so much melted in the modern systems that most of the time we, as modern lawyers, are unaware of the remote origin of concepts like "person" or "obligation," that we use every day. Through our modern vocabulary alone, it is fascinating to observe the permanence of this ancient legal system.

When I was a student of business law and patent law, I came to study the history of law through pure curiosity. Roman law attracted me, but I was much more attracted by archaic Roman law than by late Roman law, which I found was closer to our way of seeing the world. On the contrary, I sensed that archaic Roman law conveyed a different philosophy of life and another approach to justice and I believed that my professors would open up the gates of this philosophical universe for me. However, at the end of my studies in ancient Roman law, I remained unsatisfied and perplexed. My professors just laughed at archaic Roman law without, in my opinion, understanding its essence. I wondered how the most famous authorities on Roman law could consider the ancient Romans to be primitive people whom they made fun of and at the same time brilliant lawyers they admired. The most basic common sense led me to believe something was wrong. But at that time, I could not understand what and why, and I forgot all about it. Believing I had finished with the study of ancient law, as the theme of my doctoral thesis I chose the then emerging issue of the legal protection of computer software. In fact I had not finished at all with ancient Roman law, I was just beginning. The subject I had chosen led me to do research into the basis of the French legal system and especially about the fundamental distinction the French system (and many other systems) contains. It is the fundamental distinction between real rights and personal rights. As I was researching in old books for information on this issue, I was surprised to discover that modern legal systems still contain an enigma. I could see that many scholars unsuccessfully tried to solve it, and finally decided to abandon this quest that they considered to be the most sterile field in legal research. This enigma intrigued me, and I decided to follow the quest that had been abandoned a long time ago. In order to solve this enigma, I realized that it was necessary to go back to the Roman roots of our modern distinction between real rights and personal rights, which no scholar has ever done. By questioning the origins of our modern distinction when legal positivism forces us to think only about positive law, I broke the rules of that University "holy cow".

Instead of being burnt at the stake according to the ancient Parisian academic custom, I was only barred from the University, the research centers and professional publications. This finally gave me all the freedom of mind to deepen my research and the freedom of speech to publish this book.

Going back to the root of the problem made it very easy to solve the famous enigma. In turn it opened wide the gates of the philosophical horizon I would have loved to discover at the beginning of my studies of ancient Roman law. Then I understood that the special archaic intelligence, transparent in archaic Roman law had escaped the modern specialists because they were too much imbued with our materialist approach to the world. Unlike us, the ancient Romans did not observe the material world alone, they also explored the virtual world. They had understood that the virtual and the material world do not work the same way. Being practical people, they took this fact into account to invent their legal system. Today their experience has become valuable for a modern world that is rediscovering the value of ideas and the wealth of a people, who have been eclipsed by materialism for too long.

x

INTRODUCTION

Our Law and its philosophy have been conceived for an economic world where the main source of wealth was material. Although this world no longer exists, its laws are still alive and slow down the development of modern economies. Patent law strikingly shows this fact. Invented mainly during the industrial revolution in order to protect tangible inventions, it could not be applied to the new intangible inventions of the 20th century. Software, for example, has been denied protection under patent law, due to its lack of materiality. Since such a cause of denial is economically absurd, we should adapt patent law to the virtual world. This was not done and so no new intangible invention can benefit from this protection through a lack of tangibility. Long before us, the ancient Romans had understood that the virtual world and the material world do not function the same way. Since they were very practical people, they took this reality into account to build their legal system. Their legal experience has become valuable for a modern world that is rediscovering the value of ideas and the people's wealth, too long eclipsed by materialism.

In the first part, we shall present the theories that were proposed to determine the nature of the inventor's right. In the second part, we shall explain why it is impossible to answer the question of the nature of the inventor's rights without solving what the scholars have come to call the "enigma of rights". We shall see that this enigma is linked to the ancient Roman distinction between *actio in rem* and *actio in personam* and that solving the enigma allows a better understanding of the functioning of the modern patent system.

PART 1

WHAT KIND OF RIGHTS DOES AN INVENTOR HAVE? THE ANSWER FROM SOME SCHOLARS

Anna MANCINI

CHAPTER 1

The inventor's right belongs to a new category of rights

While the 1791 French Patents Act considered the inventor's right to be a right of property, the Patents Act of July 5, 1844 did not answer this question, then considered to be too metaphysical and consequently useless.

The 19th century learned opinion was favorable to the idea that inventors had a right of property. Later on, this opinion was criticized by scholars and abandoned in case law. Instead of the right of property of the inventor, two new lines of thought emerged concerning the nature of the inventor's right. The first line followed the traditional classification of rights in order to determine the nature of the inventor's right; while the second line created a new class of rights for the inventors.

While traditional law recognized two categories of rights, i.e., real rights and personal rights, many authors have claimed the need to create a new category of rights in order to classify the inventor's right. Some authors proposed considering that the inventor's right was an "intellectual right". As for Kohler, he proposed his theory of "rights on intangible things", while Roubier viewed the inventor's right as a "right on clientele". Now, we are going to study the theories proposed by the authors to explain the nature of the inventor's right.

5

SECTION 1
The inventor's rights considered as "intellectual rights" or as "rights on intangible goods"

1: Kohler's theory[1] of "right on intangible goods"

According to Kohler, the inventor's right is a right on intangible goods. The theory of rights on intangible goods or on intangible rights was proposed by Kohler in 1875.[2] Doing so, he created a new distinction in the field of the real rights category by taking into consideration the intangible object of such rights. Kohler observed that the contents of the right of property and of the intangible rights both give the same possibility to use and enjoy an object.[3] He also observed that the difference between these two kinds of rights lies in their objects. The object of the right of property is a tangible thing, whereas the object of intangible rights is an intangible object, an intangible thing.

Kohler believed that an inventor was granted the right to work an invention.[4] Such right being exclusive, absolute and protected against attacks from third parties."[5] Kohler called "invention" not a product that materializes an inventive idea, but the inventive idea itself. He asserted that "inventors can and must exert their rights on the idea, the conception and not on the perishable form".[6]

In summary, according to Kohler an invention is an intangible idea and the tangible product invented is only one of the possible materializations of the innovative idea. So the inventor's rights pertain to ideas not to things.[7]

2: Picard's theory of intellectual rights[8]

According to Picard, the rights of inventors are intellectual rights. Following a description of his scientific method, the author distinguished four categories of rights based on his observations of legal facts:

-*jura in persona ipsa*: rights in the person himself,

-*jura in persona aliena*: rights on other persons,

-*jura in re materiali*: rights on material things,

-*jura in re intellectuali*: rights on intellectual things.[9]

According to the author, intellectual rights do not pertain to the category of real rights[10] because "the same legal status cannot be appropriated to both material and intellectual things, so different in their nature and origin".[11] The author found that the category of intellectual rights was a new category which was ignored by Roman lawyers who: "did not notice that a mere intellectual thing could be the object of a right."[12] This is Picard's schematic design of a right (diagram #1):

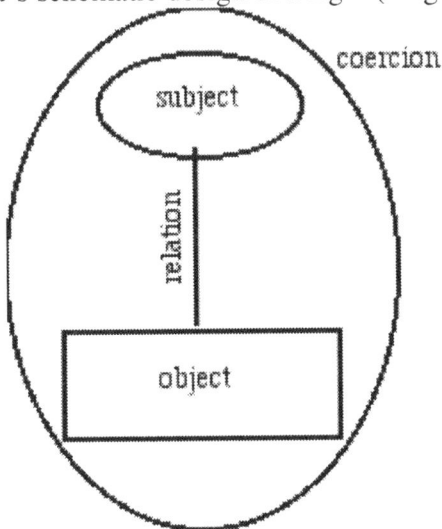

The word "subject" is for the holder of a right. The word "object" refers to the object of a right. The word "relation" is for the content of a right: "...it expresses the possible actions of the subject on the object; what the subject is authorized to do with the object, and how he can use, enjoy and transfer it."[13]

Since the author considers the content of the inventor's right to be a monopoly, while its object is an intangible inventive idea, we can schematically represent as follows the right of an inventor according to Picard (diagram #2):

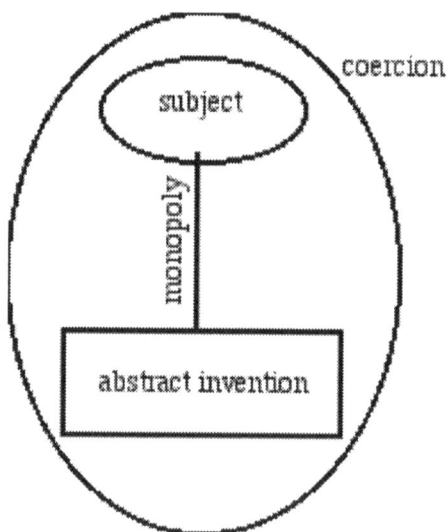

For the author, coercion (i.e., force) is the social guaranty of law, the enforcement of law. He wrote: "Law is an ideal armed with force";[14] "Without this force acting or ready to do so, law is pure Platonism".[15]

3: Dabin's theory of intellectual rights

According to Dabin, the inventor's rights are intellectual rights. Jean Dabin[16] favored the creation of a new category of rights in addition to the two existing ones created by the Romans. So, according to him, rights should be divided into three classes:
- real rights on material things,
- personal rights on persons,
- intellectual rights on intangible things (like: artistic and literary works, industrial inventions, industrial designs and patterns, trademarks, etc...).[17]

Discussing Kohler's theory, the author proposed a change of terminology. Picard believed that insofar as we traditionally accept that the expression intellectual rights means *jus in re incorporali* (right on an intangible thing), the expression Intellectual Rights is more appropriate than Kohler's expression Rights on intangible things.[18] He believed that the content of a right on intangible things is, in the case of inventions, a monopoly of exploitation.[19]

Having examined the three categories of rights, the authority concluded that the difference must be appreciated in regard of the object and not of the content of rights,[20] because whatever the right may be, its content is always a power.[21] He wrote:

"In regard of the content, the expression 'intellectual rights' is equivalent to the expressions 'real right' and 'personal right'. In regard of these three kinds of rights, there exists a certain power on various objects, with the essential difference lying in the nature of these rights".[22]

9

The author believes that intellectual rights grant a power[23] on intellectual things, an absolute power.[24]

Summarizing his thesis, Dabin[25] considered that "...intellectual rights are rights on intangible things...giving control over intangible things by appropriate means of *usus, fructus* and *abusus* (right to use, enjoy and transfer)."

For him, intellectual rights are not rights of property because property only applies to tangible things.

SECTION 2
Roubier's theory of right on clientele

According to Roubier, the inventor's right is a right on clientele. Roubier considered that the common distinction between real rights and personal rights was based upon the content of rights and not upon their objects. He wrote:

"A real right grants control over a tangible thing; a personal right corresponds to a certain credit on the debtor".[26]

Then he pointed out that the aim of the inventor's right is the conquest of clientele, that the inventor's right grants a power on clientele.[27]

In summary, Roubier distinguished three categories of rights: real rights, personal rights and rights on clientele. He explained that the third category was a new category having emerged from a new kind of society marked by trade and industry.[28]

CHAPTER 2

The right of inventors considered as a right of property

When authorities do create a new category of rights, they almost never consider the inventor's right to be a personal right. Instead, they believe that the inventor has a right of property or a right of incorporeal property.

SECTION 1:
The inventor's right of property

1: Industrial property during the French revolution

During the French Revolution, lawyers considered that inventors had a right of property on inventions. Article 1 of January 7, 1791 Act stated: "Any discovery or new invention in any field of industry is the property of its author".[29] More recently, this thesis was adopted by S. Munier.[30]

2: Munier's theory of the inventor's right of property

According to Munier, the inventor has a right of property on the invention. The author makes a preliminary distinction between economic and "personal rights" and then a hybrid distinction between real rights and personal

11

rights. She believes that the inventor's right pertains to the category of real rights, because it is an absolute and economic right. However she recognizes, as Kohler previously did in Germany, the duality of inventors rights[31] and therefore considers that the inventor's rights include moral rights (that pertain to the category of "personal rights") and economic rights (that pertain to the category of real rights). She considers the right of property to be the most absolute real right one can exert on an external thing. It allows one to benefit from all the advantages of a given thing.[32] In the author's opinion, the main feature of the right of property is the "externality" of its object with regards to the subject, while the tangible or intangible nature of the object does not matter.[33] The sole requirements for an object to be owned in the most appropriate way are "exteriority" and specification.[34]

SECTION 2
The theories of the inventor's right of incorporeal property

In 1938, Josserand was the French leader of the theory of the inventor's incorporeal property. His theory was later adopted by many authors, and it was recently developed in the field of industrial property by Mr. Mousseron.

1: Josserand's theory of the intangible right of property[35]

According to Josserand, the inventor has an intangible right of property on the invention. In 1938, Mr. Josserand observed that since the world had changed, it was now impossible to continue considering the right of property in the same way as "the primitive and simple Romans" did. He believed that the Romans had an erroneous perception of the concept of property because they believed that only a tangible thing could be the object of a right of property.[36] Also the Romans viewed the right of property not as a relationship but as "a power, a '*dominium*' (mastership)".[37]

Finally, he considered that the ancient Romans were so materialist that they considered the right of property as a right in a thing.[38]

The author's theory is built upon his criticism of the Romans' opinion according to which the right of property is a right over a given thing. But the problem is that the ancient Romans were not even familiar with the concept of "right" which is a modern invention! The author wrote:

".. it is a primitive opinion to mix property rights with their objects... the tangibility of things has no influence on the intangibility of relationships, ideas and rights around them...".[39]

We can summarize the author's proof as follows:
First step: The Romans are primitive, they mixed the right of property with its object.
Second step: A right cannot be mixed with its object, it must be separated from it.
Third step: If a right is separated from its object, then the object may be tangible or intangible.
Conclusion: A right of incorporeal property exists when the three following conditions are met: direct relationship between the good and the holder of the right; possibility to

13

draw the maximum advantages from the good; opposability to everyone for the right over the good.[40]

The author believes that since the inventor's right meets all three above-mentioned conditions, it is a right of incorporeal property.[41] He observes the tendency of the property right to be severed from its object, to be idealized and to cease being a *dominium* (i.e., a physical domain) to become a right".[42]

He points out that the right of incorporeal property is a fragile right. He says: "Since it has been considered to be less material, property has become more fragile".[43] The author considers that different kinds of property exist.

Observations on the author's method: This apparently scientific and logical method is in reality a kind of magical thinking. Did you ever meet a thing containing a right? And if extraordinarily the answer is yes, how did you separate the right from the object? If you magically succeeded in severing a right from its object, you would get, as the author stated, a fragile right instead of the strong "primitive" Roman physical power over a tangible thing.

2: Mousseron's theory of the patentee's incorporeal property

Mousseron developed his theory in 1961, in a book entitled: *The patentee's right, contribution to an objective analysis* (Le droit du breveté d'invention contribution à une analyse objective).[44] The author points out that it has become necessary to consider the patentee instead of the inventor, because from a legal and practical point of view the patentee is more important than the inventor.[45] According to the author, the patentee has become the leading character in the patent system and the first subject of the rights on inventions.[46] Mousseron believes that the object of an invention is "a new industrial result".[47] Being a "new industrial result", the invention is a good having an economic value that we can own. "Useful and rare, the new industrial result has the typical features of an economic value".[48]

Having drawn up the definitions of the subject and object of the inventors' right, the author studies how the patentee's rights are created. He observes that at the time he files a patent application, the applicant has an exclusive possession of the invention.[49] Then he notices that as patents are granted without previous examination, the patent office does not grant a right but only recognizes an existing right.[50] In other words, the patent delivery is a simple statement of an existing legal status[51] whose "aim is only the ascertainment of a previous situation".[52] The effect of a patent delivery is... "to suppress a practical or legal impediment to the exercise of a previously existing right".[53]

The author refuses to consider the patent as a privilege,[54] a contract between inventors and society[55] or a right on clientele. He describes the patent application as giving rise to the inventor's right as a unilateral legal act[56] setting up a right insofar as the invention being an intangible thing needs "a formulation in order to be identified".[57] The author believes that the patentee's right on the invention is

15

a right of incorporeal property because of the existence of the right to use, transfer, and draw profit.[58] So the patentee's right over an invention is "an absolute right directly applied to an invention, which is a movable intangible good".[59]

In Mr. Mousseron's opinion, the intangible nature of the invention does not impede the existence of a right of property, because the concept of the right of property has evolved. It no longer implies a "physical control over a solid tangible thing"[60] and the doctrine has severed the right of property from its object. In summary, the author considers that the patentee's right is a right of incorporeal property[61] because the patentee has the right opposable to all, to use, to transfer and to draw profits.[62]

In conclusion, the creation of new categories of rights is a recent evolution in law. Since the beginnings of Continental law until the turn of the twentieth century, there were only two categories of rights: personal rights and real rights. The increasing wealth created by innovative ideas (technical, scientific, artistic or literary) raised many new questions and led the scholars to write about the way we should classify the rights of creative people, especially of inventors. Today, many scholars admit the existence of three categories of rights: real rights, personal rights and intellectual rights. At the same time the concept of incorporeal property is also admitted, and even used in the French Civil Code.[63] If we want to understand the nature of the inventor's right we must necessarily understand why there is a distinction in our positive law between real rights and personal rights. This distinction is fundamental but it constitutes what the scholars have come to call the "enigma of classification between real rights and personal rights". In fact, nobody knows exactly the reason for this distinction despite the many studies on the subject. If we really want to understand the dynamics of patent law in order to better deal with innovation, we must understand the roots of our modern distinction between real rights and personal rights. Yet this distinction comes from the ancient Roman distinction between *actio in rem* and *actio in personam*. So as to be able to accurately determine the nature of the inventor's right, we must understand why the ancient Romans distinguished between *actio in rem* and *actio in personam*. Until now nobody has discovered the reason for this distinction. Scholars called this "the enigma of the distinction of rights". It gave rise to so many sterile writings that finally continental lawyers have tired of it and one of them pointed out that the research into this issue were one of the "most extraordinary mistakes in the history of mankind". Consequently, he suggested abandoning this field of research.[64]

Anna MANCINI

PART 2:

SOLVING THE "ENIGMA OF RIGHTS"

Anna MANCINI

CHAPTER 1

Scholars' unsuccessful attempts

We shall see how scholars tried to solve the "enigma of the distinction of rights" and why they failed. The issue of the distinction between real rights and personal rights, called by Mr. Dabin "the enigma of rights", has often been studied by European scholars. In France, Planiol began to criticize the traditional theory of the distinction of rights in 1938. He was so successful in so doing that until today his ideas are the first thing students are taught in French law schools. Many different theories have been proposed to solve the "enigma of rights" and some authors have written good books that gather all these opinions.[65] Here we cannot discuss all of these theories and it would not be useful to do so. Instead we are going to present the theories of three authors, insofar as they illustrate the three main steps in the evolution of this issue: Pothier highlighted the Roman distinction, Planiol contested it and finally, Ginossar eliminated it.

SECTION 1
The classical theory of the distinction of rights

19th century authorities inspired by Pothier's writings[66] pointed out that the difference between real rights and personal rights was based upon the objects of rights. With the object of a real right being a tangible thing and the object of a personal right being a person. It was considered that a real right implied a direct relationship between persons and things, while a personal right implied a relationship between persons.[67]

Pothier's ideas are long-lasting references in France and he inspired the French Civil Code which states in its Article 544:
"Property is the right to use, enjoy and transfer a thing in the most absolute way provided that we do not make any prohibited use".[68]

Pothier's theory was called the classical theory of rights and was challenged by later authors.

SECTION 2
Planiol's personalist theory

Mr. Planiol and other writers have criticized the classical theory of the distinction of rights based upon the different objects of real rights and personal rights: things or persons.

According to Planiol, a right always implies relationships between persons and never creates a direct relationship between a person and a thing. In other words a right can only consist in a relationship between persons. Therefore Planiol believes that a right on a thing implies the existence of a legal relationship between people. Mr. Planiol writes: "Any right is a relationship between persons".[69] Consequently, in his opinion the characteristic of a real right is not a relationship between a person and a thing but a relationship between persons regarding a thing. He writes:[70]

"Any real right is a legal relationship established between a person as the active subject and all other persons as the passive subjects".

He believes that the same kind of obligation arises both from the personal and from the real rights. He writes:

"The obligation imposed on all the other people is purely negative: it consists of not performing actions that would disturb the peaceful possession granted by the law to the holder of the real right".[71]

Planiol's conclusion is that real rights and personal rights have the same essence of obligation. "They differ only by two specific features, one regarding the number of passive subjects, the other the object of the obligation".[72] Planiol then reaches his famous distinction according to which: the distinction between real rights and personal rights consists of the fact that a real right is an absolute right one can defend against all others, whereas a personal right can only be defended against certain persons, so it is a relative right.[73]

This opinion is now one of the first things taught at Law Schools and is never challenged. Scholars working in the field of patent law have almost never challenged this assertion, though many authors, and particularly Mr. Demogue,[74] have proved that Planiol's opinion was wrong.

23

Mr. Demogue demonstrated that all rights are simultaneously absolute and relative and that, instead, the distinction should be made in consideration of the strength of the rights. He wrote:

"Finally, there are neither absolute nor relative rights. Any right has simultaneously these two characteristics. What can only be said from a scientific point of view is that there are strong rights and weak rights, rights more or less easy to exert. All rights create obligations, yet they vary according to practical reasons".[75]

Mr. Demogue demonstrated that: if "... a personal right has a relative nature, insofar as only the debtor has to execute the obligation, it is also an absolute right because it acts by creating or ascertaining that the obligation exists vis-à-vis any third persons. The creditor is only the debtor's creditor, the fact that he is the creditor exists *erga omnes* (for everyone else); moreover, the debtor, even if he is only the creditor's debtor, must be considered by everyone as the debtor".[76]

Demogue came to the conclusion that the scientific distinction between absolute and relative rights is useless. It is only an academic distinction used to ease the study of law. He wrote:

"Actually, there is only a pragmatic distinction of rights. rights to be exerted directly on things and rights related to facts involving the existence of other persons. Rights are all rights of obligations, varying for practical reasons".[77]

Following Demogue, many authors have now recognized

that all rights are simultaneously relative and absolute but this does not explain the reason for the fundamental legal distinction between real rights and personal rights.[78] The so-called scientific reasoning used by scholars did not allow this fundamental distinction to be understood and to go into its Roman roots. All the scholars made the error of accepting the formulation of the question raised on the basis of positive law without challenging it. Asking why the Romans distinguished between personal and real rights is a nonsensical question due to the simple fact that the concept of right did not exist in Roman law. The actual distinction the ancient Romans made was the distinction between *actio in rem* and *actio in personam*. Consequently the proper question is: why did the Romans make such a distinction? The most effective way to solve this "enigma" is to use a real scientific process. Let us study what a scientific method is and how it differs from the "legal scientific method".

SECTION 3
Scholars' lack of scientific attitude

The study of the theories proposed to solve the enigma of rights did not help to answer the related question of the nature of the inventor's right. The so-called "enigma of rights" could never be resolved by the scholars because they used an ill-adapted methodology. They approached the question from the angle of modern positive law only and missed the opportunity to go to the roots of the problem. Today it is common knowledge that the distinction between real and personal rights comes from the initial Roman distinction between *actio in rem* and *actio in personam*, that was mistranslated. It is obvious that if we want to solve the enigma, we have to consider the original Roman distinction instead of the mistranslation we can now find in positive law. It is also obvious that if we want to understand the ancient Roman distinction, we must use pragmatism and observe the world in all its aspects: tangible and intangible, as this ancient people did. We must also remember that this legal distinction was created from scratch by the Roman people. Their starting point could not be substantive law insofar as they had to create law from scratch. Using the positivist methodology and philosophy, that is to say building a logical demonstration starting out from the "pure law" is useless if we want to understand the ancient Romans. We must adopt an actual scientific method and not the positivist method which is scientific only in appearance. Generally speaking, the scholarly approach to science and its methods are erroneous. Contrary to what is currently admitted in France, scientists (mathematicians, biologists) do not exclusively work with logic. If they did, they would have achieved poor scientific progress. In fact, they work with the "whole brain" using personality and feelings as well as logic, imagination, intuition and even dreams. The scientific "impassivity" the lawyers have tried to imitate in fact does not exist in the field of science. It is a mistake to believe that scientists are "impassive" people. A scientist is not an insensitive person using only a small part of his human abilities. On the contrary, scientists need more than logic to achieve important discoveries. In the field of scientific and technological innovation, imagination, sensation, intuition, dreams and logical abilities are required. Logic only is not enough. The criticism of existing scientific theories and the confrontation between theories and reality permitted (as shown by the writings of Jean Bernard, Laurent Schwartz, Jean-Claude Pecker and Jean Hamburger) to achieve great scientific progress. No such possibilities exist in the field of law where scholars are confined to the study of rules they cannot challenge or compare with reality.

Einstein said: "Imagination is the real ground for scientific germination".[79] The mathematician Laurent Schwartz explains:[80]

"One of the main features of discovery is the removal of inhibitions. Inhibitions are a component of our mental architecture that we cannot afford to destroy".

The astrophysicist Jean-Claude Pecker[81] states:

"Anybody dealing with the Universe deals with the origins and also with metaphysical concerns...We too easily believe that we are released from reality when equations and computations are correct... Are mathematics the correct language? ... Are we not prisoners of Plato and the beauty of mathematics? "
Jean Hamburger[82] declared:

"We surprisingly become aware of the fact that the observer (more precisely, the methodology used) plays such an important role that it can even change the object.... Scientific research describes not the reality, but only the results of a dialogue between the observer and reality; a dialogue in which the observer and his method are as important as reality."

27

In conclusion, we can see that positivist reasoning is not actually scientific. Therefore we propose overcoming the limitations of modern-day legal science and using a true scientific process to try to solve the "enigma of rights".

So instead of taking our modern substantive law as a starting point, we are going to observe the natural world like scientists (as the first Roman and Greek[83] lawyers did). Legal texts are not observable natural phenomena that can be in themselves the object of scientific investigation. Laws cannot be studied apart from its context, and the real world for which it was created. In other words "pure law" is an impossible reality and lawyers should not limit themselves to the study of an intangible set of rules, but they should observe the human being in his two dimensions: substance and mind (as the Romans did).

To solve the enigma, we will first make use of imagination and intuition and then compare our findings with reality and use our logical abilities. Regarding the scientific process, Laurent Schwartz wrote in an article entitled: "About mathematical discoveries":

"Everything starts at a specific time with an idea popping up in the mind. Suddenly a question arises for which we have no answer... it is quite the opposite of what we do at school where we ask students to 'demonstrate that...'".[84]

François Jacob observes a distinction between "day and night sciences". He writes:

"Day science gives place to reasoning with logically

correlated results which have the strength of certitude... Night science, on the contrary, blindly errs... What guides the mind then is not logic, but instinct and intuition...".[85]

Jean Hamburger[86] wrote:

"Biology and medicine did not only progress thanks to new instruments and observations; they evolved through the art of reasoning. Throughout the centuries, researchers have been torn between two opposing temptations: the subjective arrogance which believes it is possible to find truth only with imagination, and the passive realism which limits itself to the accumulation of observed facts and fears any cogitation. Gradually, it appeared that the most efficient method required an exact balance between the dialogue of the objective information and the imagination of the researchers".

So while only logical abilities are allowed in the field of legal research, intuition proves to be at the root of scientific research. Intuition ("in"= in, and "tueri" = to see) is defined in psychology as:

"A revelation which suddenly emerges... (and) gives direct knowledge without reasoning, and brings forth a conviction. No judgment takes place. Some people have great natural intuition".[87]

At the end of his life, the famous psychologist C.G. Jung wrote a book considered to be his will in which he presented his long experience with the phenomena of intuition and dreams. The author wrote:

"Many philosophers, artists and even scholars owe some of their best ideas to sudden inspirations popping up from

29

the unconscious.... The mathematician Poincaré and the chemist Kékulé disclosed that the starting point of their important discoveries were sudden images emerging from their unconscious".[88]
The author affirmed:

"Even the most rigorous science, such as physics, is surprisingly dependent on intuition which acts through the unconscious".[89]

Intuition is a not modern discovery of psychology, it has always existed and was more accepted and developed in ancient civilizations than in our modern world. For example, in the field of astronomy, Democritus is deemed to have intuitively guessed by 400 B.C. the actual nature of the Milky Way, and that his description was confirmed later on by Galileo who used a telescope.[90]

Today intuition, despite the fact that it is not valued is often the starting point of great scientific discoveries. Some famous scientific researchers have disclosed the important role played by intuition in their discoveries. For example, François Jacob, the biologist, revealed that he had a sudden intuition in a cinema that led him to an important discovery in the field of genetics.[91]

C.G Jung wrote: "... even a very intelligent man may severely wander through a lack of intuition or sensitivity...".[92]

This is particularly true in the field of legal research and it is this lack of intuition and sensitivity that led famous scholars to a deadlock regarding the enigma of rights.

Intuition and good sense would have led them to a simple solution to this "enigma".

We made use of our intuition when confronted with the enigma of rights. Firstly, we intuitively felt that the question raised was not the proper question and this led us to go to the root of the problem, i.e., the original Roman distinction between *actio in rem* and *actio in personam*. Then we intuitively realized that we had to observe the world with the eyes of this ancient people in order to understand them and also that this observation should not be limited to the material world. By following our intuitions it was easy to understand why the ancient Romans made a distinction between *actio in rem* and *actio in personam*, and it was consequently also easy in a second step to compare our findings with reality and to demonstrate them logically. Let us now discover the solution to the famous "enigma of rights".

31

Anna MANCINI

CHAPTER 2

Solving the "enigma of rights"

SECTION 1

The reason for the Roman distinction between *actio in rem* and *actio in personam*

Imagine you are in Ancient Rome and you must build a legal system from scratch with the aim of creating the most balanced social organization. There is no substantive law. The simplest way to do it is to observe human beings and the real world. So, you notice that:

1. The world is composed of material and intangible things.

2. Only material things can be touched and seized.

3. A person is both material (his body) and intangible (his mind). A person being both material and intangible can perceive the intangible world of ideas or agreements, relationships, promises and liabilities which are an important foundation for a legal system. The following diagram represents the results of these first observations (diagram #3):

33

The World

Tangible   Intangible

Corporeal things
+
Human body

human mind
incorporeal things
pormises
powers
obligations

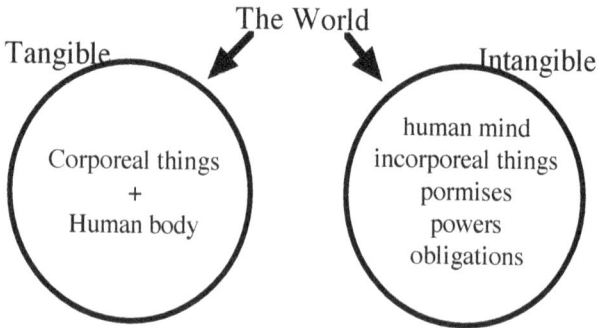

Now, we are able to draw a more precise diagram because we observed that the human being, through his body and mind, participates in both the world as material and the world as intangible. (diagram #4)

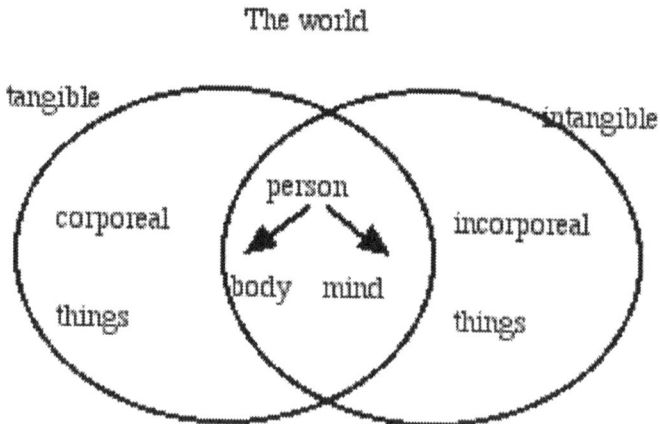

The world

tangible   intangible

corporeal

person

incorporeal

body   mind

things   things

4. A person, being both material and intangible, is able to act upon material as well as intangible things. Persons have power of action on material things: they can touch them, seize and move them, for example. They can create or give them away. At first sight, it would appear impossible to exert such a power on intangible things. But

upon closer observation, we realized that we can "act" on the intangible world functioning as a bridge between the material and the intangible. For example, through his body, a person can perceive an idea, change it, or transmit it to others through his own body.

5. For the legal world, in the case of a promise, we may notice that to obtain the performance of a promise, a person cannot directly act on the promise (take it, touch it, seize it). It is only possible to act on the promiser to make him perform his promise. So a person may act on intangible things, always through his own body or someone else's body.

In conclusion, in the context of a legal system, a person can perform:
- actions on material things (human body included);
- actions on persons (on a person's mind).

The aim of Justice is to balance conflicting human powers. The more efficient the legal system is, the more prosperous life is, personal life as well as national or international economic life. All systems of Justice should determine in each case the adequate power of each litigant. It is now easy to understand the distinction between *actio in rem* and *actio in personam*. By the *actio in rem* a litigant asked a Roman Justice: "What is my power over a material thing?" By the *actio in personam* a litigant asked a Roman Justice: "What is my power over persons to attain the intangible world?" Now we come to this diagram: (diagram #5) actio

in rem	in personam

means of action on
tangible realities

means of action on
intangible realities
through persons

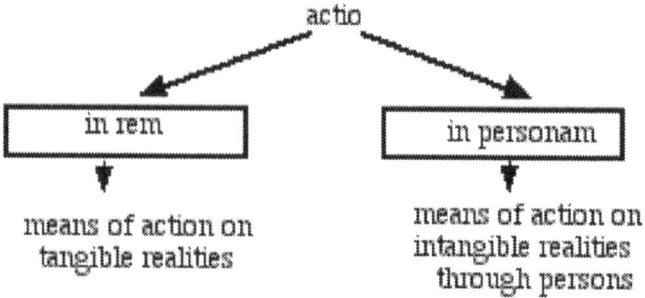

The solution to the enigma is: The Roman distinction between *actio in rem* and *actio in personam* is a consequence of natural phenomena that permit a direct action on material things (*actio in rem*) and only an indirect action on the intangible world through persons (*actio in personam*). In fact, there is a simple equation between natural phenomena and legal measures of execution and the distinction comes from a pragmatic kind of common sense.

SECTION 2
Testing the solution to the enigma

We shall now check two points:
- Is the process used valid?
- Is the solution proposed correct?

1: Is the process used valid?
Many studies confirm the validity of the process used. For example, Mr. Michas wrote:

"Roman Law had essentially a pragmatic aim, consisting of the regulation of the relationships between Romans...

the needs of current life have always inspired and penetrated Roman legal institutions".[93]

The same author quotes Mr. Van Bemmelen[94] who states:

"Abstraction was not a merit of the Romans nor one of their defects. Their legal intuition was far superior to their methodical reasoning."

Mr. Villey particularly confirms the validity of such a process. He demonstrated through many examples how the Romans observed "the nature of things". He explained that the nature the Romans observed was:

"...all that exists in our world, not only physical objects, but also the human being in his entirety; his body as well as his mind...".[95]

Mr. Villey also affirmed in a study on legal reasoning that Roman lawyers did not proceed as "scientifically" (logically) as us. He wrote:

"...today, the specialists in Roman law have established that the speech of the Roman lawyers was not scientific. 'Science', (used in its old meaning), is the speech of someone who knows, for whom certain axioms and necessary truths exist and from which necessary conclusions are drawn to build a deductive system. Euclid, for example, proceeded in a scientific way... This was not the Roman mental process. I assert that this point is unanimously accepted by specialists. This fact concerning the nature of the Roman legal discourse is emphasized in many important studies, particularly those by Fritz Schulz and Max Kaser."[96]

Mr. Aberkane naturally adopted the Romans' position. He wrote:[97]

"Depending on whether a power pertains to a tangible thing or is exerted on a person, we say it is a real right or a personal right. However, finally these powers pertain to things or persons and we cannot conceive the existence of any other element it might concern".

The author concludes: "Rationally speaking, all rights are real or personal".

Finally, it was easy to solve the "enigma" adopting a pragmatic approach. The dominant philosophy of law barred scholars from any kind of pragmatic reflection on this issue. The positivist philosophy made all the efforts of scholars sterile to solve the enigma and finally led them to abandon their quest.

Now we are able to draw the following two diagrams:
a) Diagram of human powers outside the context of a legal system (diagram #6):

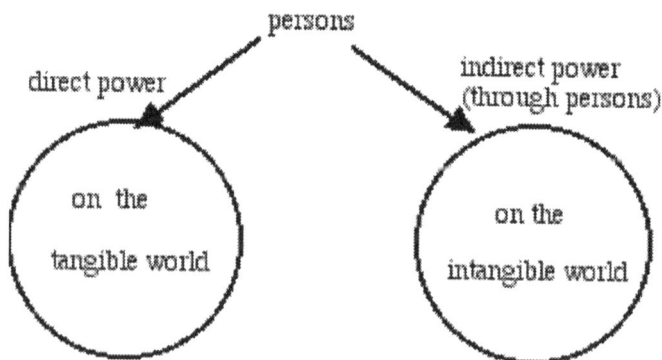

persons

direct power

indirect power (through persons)

on the tangible world

on the intangible world

b) Diagram of powers organized within the context of the Roman legal system (diagram #7):

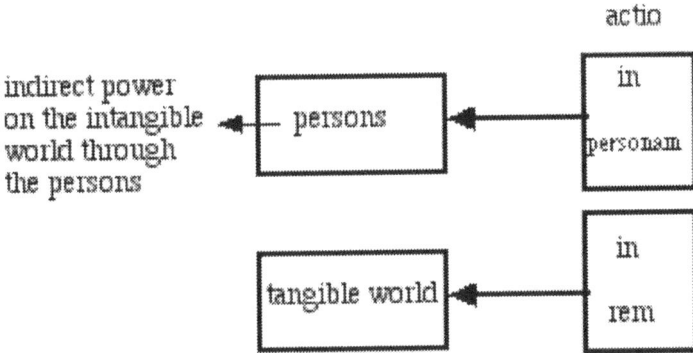

When a person had an *actio in rem,* the judge determined his power over a tangible thing. When a person had an *actio in personam,* the judge decided what power, to be exerted upon other persons, this person had over an intangible thing.

2: Control of the validity of the solution proposed

A: Comparison with the Roman world
Regarding the legal organization: In various studies we came across the idea that property is a fact. We can read in the Institutes of Justinian that property is *plena in re potestas* (full power over a thing).[98] Romans never claimed before the judge a right of property; they directly claimed the thing saying "rem meam esse" (this is my thing).[99] In effect, it is more natural and pragmatic to claim directly the thing instead of claiming a "right" over it. The modern and abstract concept of right was not known by the natural and pragmatic Romans.

Regarding possible powers: The Roman system of Justice granted only possible powers. They could not, as the French Civil Code currently does, grant an impossible direct mastership over intangible things, insofar as this was naturally impossible.[100] If the Romans heard us discussing "intellectual property" or "incorporeal property", they would laugh at us and certainly believe we are "primitive" people.

Regarding the observation of nature in Roman Law, Michel Villey quotes many examples showing that all legal acts, agreements, etc., that were impossible to perform because they were contrary to nature, were null and void in Rome.[101] He explains that any provision that was naturally impossible was legally void.[102]

Regarding the legal organization: Diagram #2 corresponds to Justinian's distinction between persons, things and actions. Mr. Michas observes the influence of Justinian's distinction on our continental legal system, especially the "famous distinction between things, persons and actions...".[103] It is suffice, however, to realize that the real world being unchanged, a classification based upon nature will last for ever.

B) Comparison with the present world
Today the measures for execution are not executed in a different way than they were in Rome, we found no other means of actions on intangible things different from acting on persons. For example, if someone "steals" an invention, the injured party never claims the return of the inventive idea, but instead asks for an injunction against the counterfeiter to cease using the invention. This is in fact

an *actio in personam* and not an *actio in rem* and the concept of property is irrelevant.

Despite the success known by the concept of incorporeal property, criminal law conflicts with the idea of stealing intangible things. In the context of criminal law, a theft implies the mastership of the stolen thing by the thief and the aim of the victim is to recover the thing. So, in the context of industrial property, it is easy to observe the impossibility to steal an inventive idea and to recover it, because we cannot touch it. Patent law never sanctions a theft, but an unlawful use of an inventive idea through an action for infringement of patent directed against persons but never against ideas.[104]

Now we are going to see how the theories proposed by scholars to explain the nature of the inventor's rights cannot stand the test of reality. Let us compare scholars' theories with reality.

Anna MANCINI

CHAPTER 3

Comparing scholars' theories with reality

In France, comparing theories with reality is uncommon in the field of legal research. More precisely, it is forbidden as the dominant philosophy of law does not allow going beyond positive law to observe reality. Even so, comparing theories with reality is the fastest and most efficient way to find whether a theory is useful or not, whereas setting up logical demonstrations often proves complex and useless. The "reality test " on scholars' theories caused them to fall down as easily as sand castles. So why continue building endless logical demonstrations severed from the real world and human needs? Let us compare the following theories with reality:
- theories creating a new kind of right for inventors (authors: Picard, Kohler, Dabin, Roubier);
- theories of the inventor's incorporeal property (i.e., intangible property) (authors: Josserand).

SECTION 1
The theories creating a new kind of right for inventors
compared with reality.

1: Picard's theory:[105]

Mr. E. Picard, a Belgian author, wrote an interesting book
at the end of his life entitled *"Le droit pur"* (*Pure Law*).
He observed the legal world and created some diagrams
which proved useful even though we cannot always agree
with the author's results. In a first step, we will
demonstrate the fallacy in some of Picard's results, using
for this purpose the ideas and diagrams of the author and
simply comparing them with reality. We will then apply
this method to other theories. This will permit a quick
demonstration. The criticisms we will formulate are
different from those generally formulated in this field; the
reason is a difference in method and framework of
reference. We will simply apply a true scientific method
that allows going beyond substantive law to observe the
whole reality of human life.

Having analyzed the structure of a right and observed
legal facts, Picard proposed the following classification of
rights according to the possible objects of rights:[106]
- *jura in person ipsa* (rights in the persons themselves)
- *jura in persona aliena* (rights over other persons)
- *jura in re materiali* (right over material things)
- *jura in re intellectuali* (rights over intellectual things).

He represented this classification in the following
diagram:[107] Diagram of the classification of rights
according to their objects (diagram #8)

personal rights   coercion   obligational rights

subject

real rights   intellectual rights

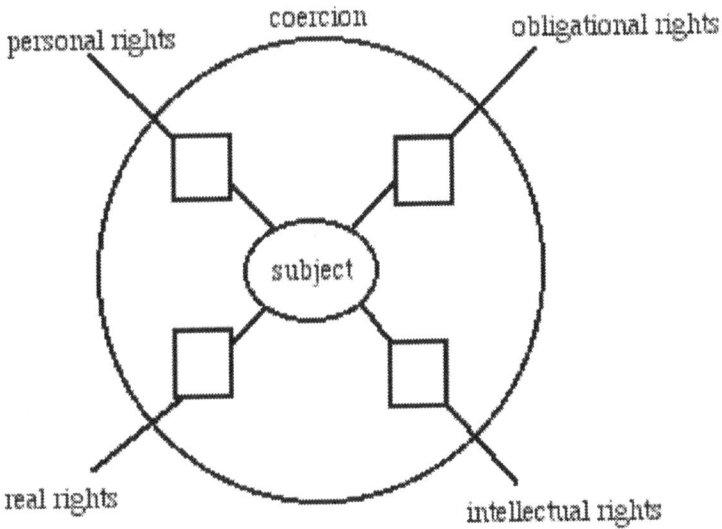

The author considers a right to be: "... a relationship of enjoyment, protected by social coercion, between a subject and an object".[108]

But as the author often considered this relationship to be a power, we can replace the "relationship of enjoyment" which is less accurate, by the word "power" which gives a clearer explanation of the relationship between a subject and an object. So we can modify the author's diagram as follows (diagram #9):

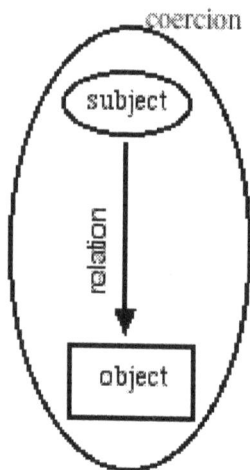

PICARD'S DIAGRAM   MODIFIED DIAGRAM

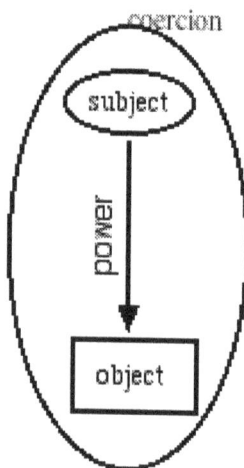

Regarding the different components of real rights he wrote:

"The object is not involved, but rather only the relationship which is divided"[109]

and he drew a diagram representing the different possible strengths of a legal relationship. Regarding the rights over other persons, he wrote:
"They consist of a more or less extended authority that may be exerted against others, from the simple credit to the father's authority."[110]

Analyzing the elements of Picard's diagram we found that:
-The circle is for social coercion, that is to say a social guaranty expressed or virtual and which leads to execution

against tangible things.

-The vertical lines are for symbolic representations of the contents of different rights. According to the author, these contents vary according to the rights:

- the content of "intellectual rights" is a monopoly;[111]
- the content of real rights is a power the intensity of which varies according to the real rights involved: right of property or simple real right;
- the content of the right of property is a full power over a thing; this content is the most powerful relationship[112] in this framework;
- the content of other real rights: other real rights resulting from the division of the right of property give rise to a relationship less powerful than the one permitted by the whole real right of property.[113] All this is easier to understand through diagrams. Diagram representing the distinction between right of property and real rights (diagram #10):

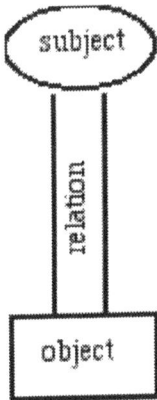

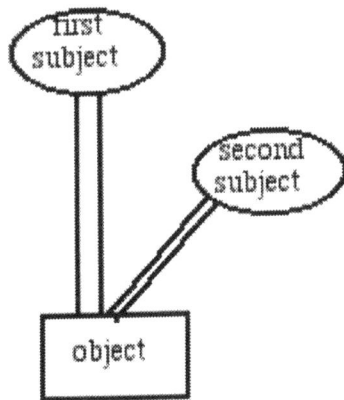

Full right   Divided right

- the content of rights over other persons is according to the author: various influences we may have over a

person;[114]
- the content of personal rights is citizenship;[115]
Subjects are for the holders of rights.

Objects are for the different possible objects of rights. For the author, they may be persons, tangible or intangible things.

We can now add the contents and complete Picard's diagrams as follows (diagram #11):

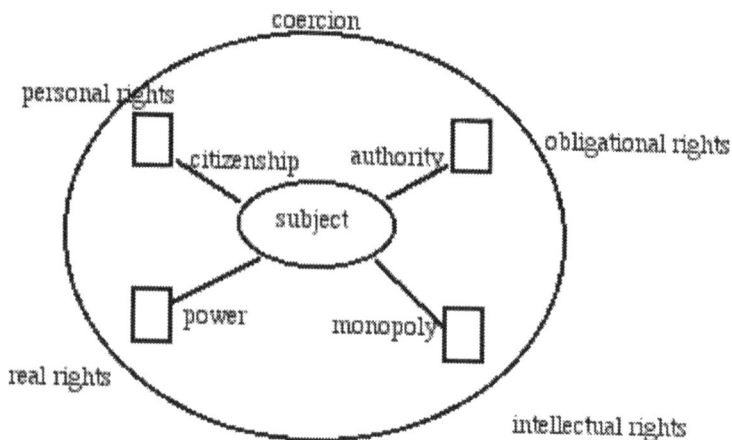

We wonder why the author did not consider the content of all rights as a same power varying in intensity, insofar as this idea of "power" is ever present in the author's writings. Didn't he analyze the divisions of the right of property as weaker powers?[116] It is surprising to notice that the new category of intellectual rights is simply qualified as a "monopoly".

Through the author's diagrams it appears that social coercion must be moved against the objects of rights, and

that:
- In the event of an attack on a real right, coercion should bear on a material thing.
- And in the event of non-compliance with intellectual rights, coercion should apply on intellectual things.

If we consider the inventor's right, the object of which is the invention, we must admit, according to the author's theory, that coercion should be applied over an invention. In effect, the author's writings reveal that coercion can only be exerted on the objects of rights.

Having examined the objects on which coercion is applied according to Mr. Picard's ideas, we know that coercion must bear only on the objects of rights. This means that for intellectual rights coercion may be exerted upon inventive ideas. We must realize that such a guaranty of intellectual rights would be useless in practice and, moreover, impossible. It is obvious that an efficient coercion must apply to persons infringing the inventor's monopoly in the case of intellectual rights. The "monopoly", as classified by the author, is guaranteed by states allowing the inventor to prevent all other persons from working with the patented invention. In the event of an attack on the inventors' right, it would be nonsense to exert coercion on the invention, but more sensible to exert it against counterfeiters. Summarizing our observations regarding the exercise of coercion, we notice that coercion can only be performed against tangible objects or against people and we find again the initial Roman distinction between the two categories of measures for execution *actio in rem* and *actio in personam*.[117] The measures available nowadays for execution still involve persons or

49

things. There is nothing else new because nature does not permit it. We cannot seize an idea, an obligation or a duty,[118] and the author wrote: "Without social coercion, law is pure Platonism".[119]

So we should remember that:

- contents of rights are always powers recognized and guaranteed by law;
- a right considered as a power is not only a relationship between persons, but also a relationship between tangible things and persons. This point was largely demonstrated by Mr. Picard;
- insofar as all rights are socially guaranteed powers. In practice it is important to determine the objects of such rights with the aim of instituting the most efficient guaranty. By doing so, we again find the Roman classification: tangible things, persons and legal actions (guaranties of possible powers).

The Romans distinguished between tangible and intangible things.[120] Insofar as the Romans were very natural and pragmatic, they could not have created a useless distinction. Thus, if we do not find a legal *actio* to guaranty intangible things, the reason is simply because intangible things are guaranteed through persons and because the "direct guaranty" of an intangible thing is impossible in practice.

For the Romans, the relationships between persons were very important and initially they used "magic" to regulate them, thereby being able to bind persons or break a relationship between them. They seemed more knowledgeable than us in how to deal with man's imagination. Magic was perhaps one way to act on imagination; a way to create "intangible things" such as obligations which are invisible binding links. Roman law was particularly efficient regarding persons because it used strong psychological pressures on them. Now let us test other theories on the nature of inventor's rights proposed by the authors.

2: Criticism of Kohler's theory[121]

We can represent the author's ideas as follows (diagram #12):

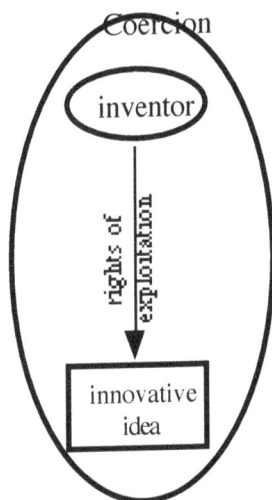

Thanks to this diagram, it is possible to point out easily and quickly that this theory is mistaken. As the object of the inventor's right is, according to Kohler, the inventive idea and as the legal coercion must be executed against the object of rights, the conclusion is that in case of infringement of the right of exploitation pertaining to the inventor, the action for infringement should be exerted

51

against the inventive idea.[122] This would be nonsense. In fact, the action for infringement can only be exerted on persons because we have no possibility to exert any coercion whatsoever on ideas.

3: Criticism of Dabin's theory about intellectual rights

There is little difference between the theories of Mr. Kohler and Mr. Dabin; only a change in terminology. Consequently, the criticism of Mr. Dabin's theory is similar to the criticism of Mr. Kohler's theory. We can represent Dabin's theory as follows (diagram #13):

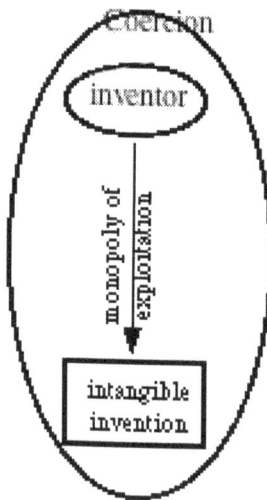

The author, in his writings, noticed that intangible things are the "less easy objects of a monopoly."[123] Nevertheless, he believed that the object of the inventor's right was the invention (or inventive idea). But, it is clear, taking into account the real world, that the object of an inventor's rights cannot be an idea because coercion cannot be exerted on it.

4: Criticism of Roubier's theory of the right over clientele

We can represent Roubier's theory of the inventor's right as follows (diagram #14):

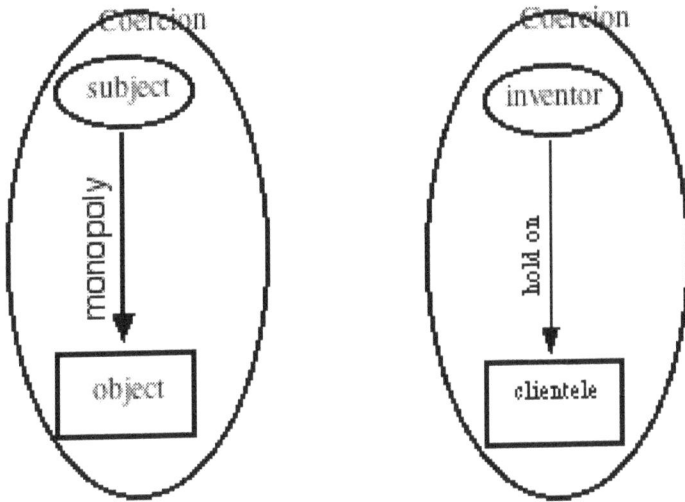

We immediately notice that a right over clientele is nonsense in an efficient legal system. Surely, if somebody infringes the patentee's right, it is useless to act against the clientele; it is preferable and more efficient to act against the counterfeiters. So the object of a patentee's right cannot be a clientele and the content of such a right cannot be a power over clientele. The truth is that a patentee is given a power over others to ensure that his right is respected.

SECTION 2
Criticism of the concept of incorporeal property

In the first paragraph, we shall see how this concept was created; in the second paragraph, we shall criticize this concept in Mr. Josserand's writings.

1: From the traditional concept of property to the concept of incorporeal property

A) Original features of the right of property
The concept of property is fundamental for the continental legal system. Many scholars have written on this matter while proposing their own classification of rights. Generally, authors distinguish between economic and non-economic rights. The right of property is considered to be an economic right; it is the "king" of the real rights. "It is the most complete right a man may exert on a thing".[124] It gives a person "an immediate and direct power upon a thing".[125] For some authors, economic rights must be divided into: real rights, personal rights and intellectual rights;[126] for others, the classification must remain traditional and they distinguish only between real rights and personal rights.[127]

The writings concerning the classification of rights give greater importance to real rights, especially to the right of property. The common opinion is that: a real right implies an "immediate and direct relationship between a thing and a person having a power, more or less strong and complete, over it";[128] and that real rights imply a relationship between the holder and well determined tangible things. Mr. Roubier[129] noticed: "Real rights ...

have been organized... according to goods of the external world".

Authors referring to the Romans observed that the right of property implied the mastership of a thing and that in Rome the transfer of property was inconceivable without the transfer of the thing itself. They stressed the fictitious nature of our modern contractual transfer of property.[130]

Originally it was not the right of property that existed but only the concept of property. Such a concept of property allowing a complete mastership over a tangible thing could also exist outside of the legal framework. Later, property became for lawyers a right of property still pertaining to tangible things.

B) The initial dematerialization of the concept of property

The fact that property became a right of property and that the contractual transfer of the right of property did not require a simultaneous transfer of the related tangible thing, was the starting point of what Mr. Josserand called the "dematerialization of the concept of property". Lawyers fictitiously severed the right of property from its object in order to facilitate the transfer of tangible goods.[131] Adding fictions to fictions, some authors came to consider that an object is not a good, with the good being on the contrary only the right pertaining to this good.[132]

C) The birth of incorporeal property

The authors' main argument was that the right of property pertains to both tangible and intangible things, because the essence of the right of property lies in its content, not in its object. Gradually a tangible object for the right of property was no longer required, so leading to the concept of incorporeal property, that is to say a property on an intangible thing. The intangible object of a right of property can be a right, an invention, an idea, etc. Regarding the concept of incorporeal property, Mr. GINOSSAR demonstrated that the right of property tends to be superimposed to all other rights. So rights, once they have become goods, it is possible to own them in the same way as we have a right of property over tangible things.

Many authors have defended the following reasoning:
1: A right has a certain value.
2: Therefore a right is a good.
3: The right of property pertains to goods.
4: If a right is a good, then the right of property may pertain to rights.
5: Conclusion: a right of property pertaining to rights is a right of incorporeal property.

Roubier wrote: "Our civil law is normally established upon the basis of material or intangible goods".[133]

But he observed that: "Thanks to the theory of the *res incorporales* (intangible things), our modern legal system goes further still. It considers as goods other rights such as obligatory rights, rights over clientele..."[134]

and he asserted that real rights can pertain to all these rights.
Another author wrote:

"The word "good" means economic right. However, we

usually distinguish between tangible goods (tangible things) and intangible goods (real rights, personal rights or intellectual rights)".[135]

Today, two meanings are recognized for the word "good": firstly, it refers to tangible things; secondly, it refers to "rights pertaining to things".[136] But the most important thing to notice is that authors use the word "good" when something has a certain value, notwithstanding its nature: material or intangible.[137]

D) Creation of new objects that can be owned
The last step in the "evolution" of the right of property consisted of creating new kinds of things to be owned. These new things are neither rights nor tangible things; they are intangible things such as inventive ideas or artistic ideas. Kohler called them intangible goods. The logical legal demonstration is now obvious and easy:
1: An idea has a certain economic value.
2: Therefore an idea is a good.
3: Since it is a good, an idea can be owned.
4: Conclusion: there is "a right of intellectual property".
The demonstration seems logical but practice is reluctant to such logic. Several authors using an economic vocabulary demonstrated that an inventive idea being useful and rare was a good having a certain value and that such a good could be owned. But Mr. Adda recently noticed some practical problems that were not mentioned by the above logical demonstration, for example: how is it possible to apply to an idea a clause of reservation of property (Adda took the example of software)?[138] How can the continental theory of concealed defects be applied to an idea? This theory was elaborated for material things

and led to distinguishing between conspicuous defects and concealed defects.

In the software example, people never try to prove that software (an intellectual good) contains a concealed defect; they only demonstrate the non-performance of the supplier's duty. The question involves persons not matter, and the theory of concealed defects is irrelevant for intangible goods.

Summary of the evolution of the concept of property from material property to incorporeal property

1) In the beginning, there was no right of property but only property mixed with its object. Without the transfer of a tangible thing a transfer of property was impossible. The birth of the right of property made it possible to transfer a right of property without transferring at the same time the tangible thing to which it pertained. This contractual transfer of the right of property was the starting point for the further separation between the right of property and its object. Such a separation allowed lawyers to focus their attention on the content of the right to the detriment of its object. The content was considered to be more important that the object, the doctrine declared that the right of property bore on tangible things as well as on intangible things such as rights, or ideas. Such a doctrine gave birth to the concepts of rights of incorporeal property and of intellectual property. Nowadays, the concept of incorporeal property is widely admitted in doctrine and in practice and Mr. Catala wrote:

"For a long time, the concept of property without a tangible object shocked people used to the Roman theory

58

of rights. Wasn't the essence of property a tangible thing, the object of this right? But recent studies have shown that the main feature of the right of property is the absolute opposability to all...".[139]

2: Criticism of Josserand's theory of incorporeal property[140]

The starting point for Mr. Josserand's demonstration is the criticism of a non-existent Roman right. The author believed that "primitive and trivial Romans mixed things and the right of property", that they did not know about the concept of right and that to them property was more a power over a thing than a legal relationship.[141]

Mr. Josserand believes that we must not mix the right of property with the thing. In Mr. Josserand's opinion, the right of property must be distinguished from its object so that: "..the right of property being dematerialized and idealized can bear on intangible things, and not only on tangible things.... The right of property gives a power over its object without being identified with it".[142]

Consequently, he considers that a patentee has a right of incorporeal property over his inventive idea. This opinion can be schematically represented as follows (diagram #15):

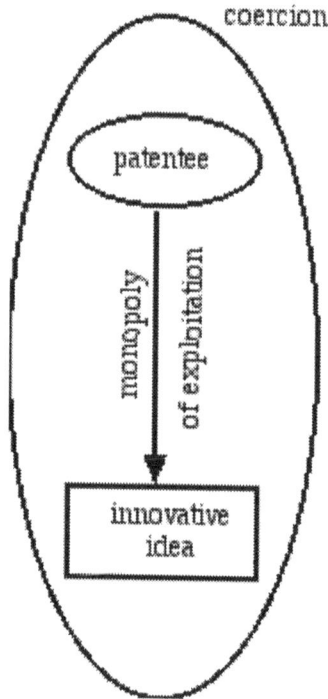

It is easy to notice that in the case of an attack on the monopoly of exploitation, coercion should be brought to bear on the object, more precisely, on the inventive idea. This is impossible in practice.

So, in conclusion, the right of incorporeal property over an inventive idea is certainly a very modern conception, but it is useless in practice. So Mr. Josserand wrote:
"From the fact that it has become less material, property has become more fragile".[143]

In fact, having a right of property over an intangible inventive idea is not useful in practice because, as we have seen, social coercion is always exerted on the objects of rights. In the case of patent law, it is clear that coercion is never exerted against inventive ideas but against people who infringed on the inventor's monopoly. In fact, the objects of rights can only be tangible things and people. As in ancient Rome, to reach the intangible -in the case of patent law, the innovative idea- we have no other means than to act upon the persons so that they will respect the monopoly conferred to the patentee. From all that it results that the patentee's right is not an intellectual right or a right of incorporeal property, but simply a personal right. The solution to the enigma of rights makes it clear. Let us now see how, prior to becoming a right of property, the inventor's right was regarded as a privilege, i.e., a personal right.

PART 3

THE ANSWER TO THE NATURE OF THE INVENTOR'S RIGHT LIES IN ANCIENT ROMAN LAW

Anna MANCINI

CHAPTER 1

Inventors and privileges

We know from the solution to the enigma of rights that we can reach the intangible only through persons. Inventive ideas are intangible things that can only be reached through people, therefore the right of an inventor can only be a personal right. So we can now draw the following diagram of the inventor's right (diagram #16):

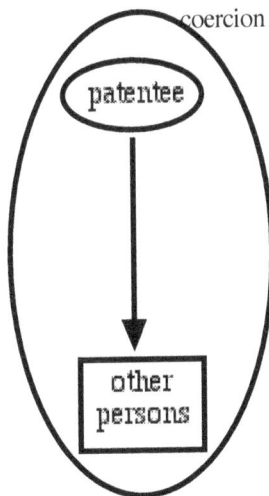

The power the inventor has over other people consists of forbidding them to do something. The French Act of January 2, 1968 (new text - Article 29, and the following ones) contains a list of prohibitions as follows:

Article 29:
"The patent shall confer on its owner the right to prevent all third parties not having his consent:
a) from making, offering, putting on the market or using a product which is the subject matter of the patent, or importing or stocking the product for these purposes;
b) from using a process which is the subject matter of the patent or, when the third party knows, or it is obvious in the circumstances, that the use of the process is prohibited without the consent of the owner of the patent, from offering the process for use on French territory;
c) from offering, putting on the market, using, or importing or stocking for these purposes the product obtained directly by a process which is the subject matter of the patent".[144]

In fact, the Act simply allows a privilege to the patentee and a privilege is a personal right. Before the French revolution this fact was admitted in law, let us see why it was no longer admitted later.

The word "privilege" used for inventors' rights is today often found in writings to qualify such rights

SECTION 1
The survival of the word privilege

Concerning the legal nature of a patentee's rights, we often read: "monopolies of exploitation" "opposable to all". But what is in reality a monopoly of exploitation opposable to all? It is simply a privilege. Authors sometimes use this expression when arguing in favor of the right of incorporeal property thesis.

An author simply affirmed: "Obviously the State is sovereign. As it is the State which grants patents, ... it may also suppress this privilege and grant only a reward or an equitable remuneration to the inventor."[145]

Mr. Wagret considered the patent to be an "economic privilege".[146] Mr. Isore noticed:

"What are our modern patents, but privileges granted with a purpose of social interest."[147]
The word privilege has often been used in case law and some decisions have clearly mentioned that no right of property exists but only a privilege. A Supreme Court (Cour de Cassation) judgment, dated July 25, 1882 (which concerned authors' rights, but can be applied to the subject) declared:

"Whereas authors' rights and the monopoly they confer are wrongly called property in legal or usual language; they are far from being a property as described and organized by the Civil Code for movable and immovable goods. They only grant their holders an exclusive and temporary privilege of exploitation."[148]

67

Another case dated December 22, 1936 stated:

"The delivery of a patent appears to be an act of government, something like a sovereign act".[149]

In a decision dated August 11, 1836 we read:[150]
"If, instead of a new discovery, the would-be inventor gives to society only a discovery already known that can be found in published and printed books, the would-be inventor is therefore barred from getting a patent..."[151]

A decision of the Court of Paris dated February 1, 1900, concerning musical creations viewed rights on musical creation as "exclusive privileges of exploitation".[152] Today, cases often use the expression "monopoly of exploitation"[153].
Despite the fact that previously the inventor's rights were considered to be a privilege, i.e., personal rights, scholars have been reluctant to explore the category of personal rights and to regard inventors' rights as personal rights, since the French Revolution. Let us see why this occurred.

CHAPTER 2

Why scholars ignored the category of personal rights

In the first section, we shall explain how the misunderstanding of the Roman distinction led authors to mistake the main feature of the modern right of property and how this mistake prevented them from better exploring the category of personal right. In the second section, we shall show a second reason why authors did not explore the "personal field": the considerable long-lasting attraction in continental lawyers' minds of the concept of right of property.

SECTION 1
The mistake regarding the main characteristic of real rights

The positivist philosophy of law confined scholars to substantive law which did not allow them to resort to the Roman roots of the modern "enigma of rights". Scholars could not compare their theories with practice. The dominant philosophy of law only allowed them to analyze, compare and discuss substantive law using their logical mind. As a result of their confinement to the study of positive law, the reason for the modern distinction of rights remained an "enigma". In fact, without going back to its Roman roots, it was impossible to solve this enigma and to understand the actual difference between real rights and personal rights. Also for scholars fascinated by the concept of property, it was difficult to spend more of their time exploring the category of personal rights and to understand its dynamics which is so important to the modern economic world. Let us show how much scholars are fascinated by the right of property.

SECTION 2
The fascination of scholars for the right of property

The right of property is the most frequent topic studied by continental lawyers and philosophers. They wonder about its basis, justification, social function, utility and about the role played by the State in regard to private property. Studies on the right of property have increased with the emergence of the concepts of incorporeal property and intellectual property. Even authors in the field of criminal law have seriously discussed the possibility of stealing intangible things like ideas. The increasing economic value of ideas considered to be "goods" is giving rise to an increasing number of continental studies on the concept of property.[154]

1: The modern charm of the right of property

Since "intangible goods" are becoming increasingly valuable, scholars believe that the best way to protect this new kind of wealth is through the right of property. In their opinion, the right of property is the most appropriate right due to the security it provides. The right of property is deemed to be better guaranteed by social coercion than the personal right which is considered to be weak. Mr. Terré wrote:

"Every legal field wants to have its own right of property, because this right is the symbol of an absolute legal protection".[155]

On the contrary, Catala[156] and Roubier [157] wrote about the growing weakness of the personal rights since the Roman era.

In conclusion, three main points prevented the authors from exploring the field of personal rights:

- the positive philosophy of law confining them to the study of law and prohibiting them from testing realities;
- the persistent and erroneous belief that absoluteness is the main characteristic of the right of property whilst relativity is the most important characteristic of personal rights;
- the fact that continental lawyers have a long-lasting fascination for the right of property to the detriment of personal rights. This fascination was strong during the French Revolution (in 1789) and the legislator made use of it to help maintain the inventor's rights. Let us now see why, during the French Revolution, the inventor's privilege was transformed into a right of property.

2: Why the inventor's privilege became a right of property during the French Revolution

A) The situation of creators before the revolution
Inventors and artists in older days already benefited from

favors or privileges.[158] Mr. Vivant[159] wrote that in Athens, in the sixth century B.C, there was a law granting a privilege to a new gastronomic specialty. This privilege consisted of being the sole user of this culinary invention for one year.

In France, privileges for literary and artistic works were not necessarily granted to the authors originally and were, on the contrary, arbitrarily delivered to booksellers. A slow evolution towards greater equity began approximately in 1579 and led, step by step, to a regulation of the terms and conditions for the attribution of privileges and to the attribution of the privilege to authors.

As regards industrial creations, they were protected in England as early as 1623 by the Statute of Monopolies.[160] In France, privileges began to be recognized by branches of industrial activities. They were often confirmed, as from May 4, 1548, but were generally granted to trade guilds and rarely to inventors.[161] Inventors had to wait until the Revolution for the abolition of the trade guilds and for the direct recognition of their rights.

During the French Revolution, the inventor's right of property was created under pressure from the inventors involved, who claimed the recognition of their rights in 1790 before the National Assembly (Assemblée Nationale).

B) The right of property for inventors in the revolutionary law of January 7, 1791

When studying this text, it is clear that the inventors were granted a right of property because it would not have been politically correct to maintain their privileges. In effect, during the night of August 7, 1790 all privileges were abolished in France, therefore the word privilege (even granted equitably) could not reasonably be used in a law after such abolition. The word "property" was much more suitable and surer for helping to preserve the existing inventors' privileges. Mr. Roubier noticed that the revolutionaries wanted to make sure that the rights conferred to inventors would be accepted, so they did not call them "privilege" but rather "property".[162] Obviously, the inventor's rights were privileges as they are today. Mr. Berville wrote on the correlative field of authors' rights:

"Writers' rights are not rights of property. The word property used by the legislator is a polite word, but it is not a legal definition".[163]

Article 7 of the Act of January 7, 1791 is clear enough about the motivation of the French government during the Revolution:

"The National Assembly does not want to attack the exclusive privileges already granted for inventions and discoveries, ...they remain valid...".[164]

Calling the rights of the inventors: "right of property" was a historical necessity, which permitted the survival of inventors' privileges under the mask of property. But we must remember that the concept of "inventors' right of property" was a fiction and that, in reality, these rights were only privileges granted when certain conditions were met. We can read in the preamble of the law:

"The National Assembly, considering that any new idea,

73

the manifestation or development of which may become useful to society, is firstly owned by its finder and that not to consider an industrial discovery as being its author's property would constitute an infringement on the essence of human rights".[165]

SECTION 2
Roman wisdom for patent law

In its beginnings patent law mainly dealt with industrial and mechanical inventions. Nowadays new kinds of inventions raise insoluble questions for lawyers. Lawyers wonder whether they should protect them under patent right or create a specific law for every new intangible invention. This occurred regarding software which was considered to be impossible to patent due to its intangibility. After long discussions worldwide on this issue, it was decided to protect software using copyright law. In fact, any new kind of "intangible invention" will cause new problems for lawyers and new international tensions regarding the way they should be protected. This is why we thought it was important to clarify the philosophy of patent law with the help of Roman wisdom and pragmatism in order to modernize patent law so that it will be an advantage for modern economy instead of a drawback. Patent law must recover its original pragmatism.

1: Patent law must recover its original pragmatism

When studying the history of patent law we can see that in the beginning the conditions the inventor had to meet to get a patent were very simple: he had to bring new knowledge to society and be the first to do so in the country. The law considered an invention to be a "new idea", a "discovery" and the legislator clearly indicated that "new ideas and discoveries the manifestation or development of which may be useful to society"[166] were patentable. The criterion of social utility was central, the 1791 Act was pragmatic and its preamble full of economic considerations:

"The National Assembly considers that any new idea the manifestation or development of which may become useful to society, primarily belongs to its finder, and that it would be an infringement on the essence of human rights, not to regard an industrial discovery as its author's property....
Taking also into account, how much the lack of such declaration... may have contributed until now to discourage French industry, causing the emigration of several distinguished artists, and allowing a great number of new discoveries to pass to foreign countries ...".[167]

The same law granted patents to: "...any first person bringing a foreign discovery" (article 5).[168]

Article 2 of the 1791 Patent Act has to be considered with a wide meaning allowing to grant a patent for any "invention" economically useful, even when it is not, strictly speaking, an invention (Article 2: "Any means adding a new kind of improvement to whatever fabrication shall be considered to be an invention").[169]

The 1791 Patent Act set forth in a few lines what was a

patentable invention. Social utility and economic interests were central in the determination of patentability. Modern patent law is no longer focused on this clear, pragmatic and simple economic aim, but has developed a complex set of conditions to be met by an invention so that an inventor can obtain a patent. So we can observe that instead of focusing on the original aim of patent law which was to promote technical, industrial and economic growth, lawyers now only discuss the characteristics a product must meet in order to be patentable. According to present criteria for obtaining a patent, an invention (an inventive idea) is patentable only if its manifestation or development is tangible. So in accordance with such criterion, an invention of high economic utility but the object of which is considered to be intangible cannot be patented. Such was the case of software. Though patentability should logically have been recognized on the economic grounds for software, patentability was denied to software because lawyers considered software to be intangible and consequently impossible to patent. Instead of considering if pragmatically it would have been the right economic solution to recognize the patentability of software, lawyers asked themselves this kind of questions: "Is software an artistic and literary work?" "Is it a kind of language creation?" "Does it meet the patentability requirements?"

The same occurred regarding semi-conductor chips But lawyers' sterile reflections about the legal nature of semi-conductors were soon aborted by American pragmatism. The American authorities quasi obliged Europeans to quickly adopt a specific protection for semi-conductor chips.[170] This was done in France by the Act of

November 4, 1987 which refers to several provisions of the French Patent Act (Articles: 40-43-44-46-59-67-68).[171] The issue of software and semi-conductor chips showed how much the right granted to their inventors by the States was a privilege and not a right of property. In effect, a specific privilege was created for semi-conductor chips and despite the technical nature of software, governments worldwide decided to grant the literary and artistic privilege to the inventors of the software. Software is nowadays protected worldwide under copyright law. The problem the modern world has to face with present patent law is that it does not take into account the growing intangible origin of economic wealth. Patent law needs to be improved and Roman wisdom can help in this field.

2: The help of Roman law to improve modern patent law

The actual nature of the rights over invention must be recognized in order to improve modern patent law and make it a more efficient tool to help economic, technical, scientific and technological development. Through solving the enigma of rights we have understood that property regards material things, while we can protect intangible things only through the category of personal rights. Since an invention is something intangible, i.e., a new idea, the best way to protect its inventor is to grant him a personal right which allows him to prohibit all other people from working with the invention protected and to materialize and commercialize his inventive idea. Despite the application of the concept of incorporeal property to the inventor's right, patent law finally grants a monopoly

77

to the patentee, in other words a privilege, a personal right and it is time to clearly recognize this.

In order to have an efficient patent system we need to accurately classify the inventor's rights. For this purpose, ancient Roman wisdom is essential to the modern economy. Primitive civilizations were not as much focused on the material world as the modern world. They also took into account the intangible world and observed the connection between the tangible and the intangible. With the growing economic value of intangible goods, lawyers are facing new problems raised by the fact that positive law (patent law included) was conceived for an economic world dominated by material wealth. Positive law is not suited to intangible wealth and cannot help promote economic growth based on intangible goods. Ancient Roman wisdom is more useful in this respect, because ancient Roman lawyers had already observed the dynamics of the intangible world and organized the legal impact on the intangible. Solving the enigma of rights led to recovering their knowledge on this aspect and made it available to modern lawyers. The modern economic world is shifting from the preeminence of material wealth to that of wealth coming from the intangible, mainly from people's creativity. Due to the increasing wealth originating from creativity, the category of personal rights is called to come to the first place of the legal and economic stage. Throughout history lawyers have found it useful to apply the concept of property to the field of invention, but nowadays such an attitude is detrimental to the economy. It has obscured the reflection on this issue and led scholars to focus their attention on the protected objects of the inventions so much, that finally they forgot to consider the relationship taking place between people regarding innovation. They also forgot the original purpose of patent law: economic, scientific and technical growth. Modern lawyers should urgently reconsider the personal dimension of the patent system and stop focusing their attention on patentable objects. Any kind of invention, whether or not it gives rise to the creation of a tangible good, should be protected under patent law provided it is useful to society and the economy. The main purpose of patent law should be, as in its beginning, to balance the relationship between people, in other words between the inventor's interest and the interests of society.

Anna MANCINI

CONCLUSION

Due to its unsuitability in terms of intangible wealth, patent law is becoming contrary to economic interests and is decaying, giving rise to new "satellite" laws. The problem is that for every new "intangible" invention that is created, States will need to negotiate new international agreements and approve new national laws so losing the advantages of a well-established international patent system and wasting time in the process. It would be better to adapt patent law to make it economically reasonable and useful, remembering that:

- An invention is always an abstraction, an idea.
- States grant a personal right to inventors.
- This personal right is a privilege allowing the inventor the right to prohibit all other persons from exploiting the patented invention.
- The main purpose of patent law should be economic, scientific and technical growth.
- We cannot act directly on an intangible invention, the only way to act on the intangible is to act through persons and this is why the right of an inventor is a personal right and not a right of property.

Positivism and legal engineering are still useful for the day-to-day allocation of law, but positivism is an important source of rigidity preventing legislators from updating legal rules according to national and international realities. Positivism prohibits a sound understanding of the past and a sensible preparation of the future. The dominant legal philosophy confines scholars to the application of laws made for a material world and unsuited to the modern economy where the intangible gives rise to increasing economic wealth. Lawyers need to free themselves from the positive philosophy of law which prevents them from observing the world and confines them to the study of substantive law. How can lawyers help regulate a world they have not explored? We need, especially in the field of patent law, to recover a true legal art which should allow the creation of a living law for an expanding new scientific and technological world. Real law is art (not only technique) speaking to man's imagination as well as to man's reason. Psychology, imagination, intuition, pragmatism and reasoning skills are all needed to create the law. Legal art is a creative process, but positivism blocks the possibility of a creative adaptation of the law to the modern world. The world is changing, and the intangible world is increasingly becoming the source of economic wealth. Positive law is based on a material economy only and is ill-adapted to the modern economy. On the contrary, the wisdom of ancient Roman law, based upon the observation of the dynamics of both the material and the intangible world, is very valuable for guiding modern legislators in their creation of efficient laws.

BIBLIOGRAPHY

ROMAN LAW

Breal Michel and Bailly Anatole, *Dictionnaire étymologique latin*, Paris, Hachette, 1898

Catalano Pierangelo, *Diritto e Personne, Studi su origine e attualità del sistema romano*, Torino, G. Giapaichelli Editore, 1990

Gaudemet Jean, *Droit privé romain*, Paris, Montchrestien, 2000.

Grimal Pierre, *La civilisation romaine*, Paris, Champs, Flammarion, 1997

Guarino Antonio, *Storia del diritto romano*, Napoli, Jovene, 1998.

Huvelin Paul, *Les tablettes magiques et le droit romain*, Macon, Protat Frères, 1901

Jhering von R., *L'esprit du droit romain dans les diverses phases de son développement*, translation by O. de Meulenaere, Paris, Librairie A. Marescq, MDCCCLXXXVI.

Levy-Bruhl Henri, *Droit romain*, Paris, Cours de droit, 1955/56.

Levy-Bruhl Henri, *Le très ancien procès romain*, Rome, 1952.

Levy-Bruhl Henri, *Nouvelles Etudes sur le Très Ancien Droit romain*, Paris, Recueil SIREY, 1947.

Levy-Bruhl Henri, *Recherches sur les actions de la loi*, Paris, Recueil Sirey, 1960.

Paricio Javier, Fernandez Barreiro A., *Historia del derecho romano y su recepción europea*, Madrid, Editorial centro de estudios Ramon Areces, 1995.

Potter T. W., *Roman Britain*, London, Bristish Museum Press, 1997

Revillout Eugène, *Les origines égyptiennes du droit civil romain*, Paris, Librairie Paul Geuthner, 1912

Villey Michel:"Le jus in re du droit romain classique au droit moderne", in *Publications de l'Institut de droit romain de l'Université de Paris*, 1947, p. 193

Villey Michel, "Historique de la nature des choses", Paris, *Archives de Philosophie du droit*, volume X, 1965, p. 267-283.

Villey Michel, "Métamorphoses de l'obligation", *Archives de Philosophie du droit*, Communication au congrès de l'Institut International de Philosophie politique sur "l'obligation politique" 4 juillet 1969

Villey Michel, *Le Droit Romain*, PUF, Que sais-je?, 7e édition, 1979

Villey Michel, *Suum jus cuique tribuens*, Milano, Giuffré, 1954

Some websites

http://www.jura.unisb.de/Rechtsgeschichte/Ius.Romanum/english.html
http://www.iuscivile.com/
http://www.frankcass.com/jnls/jlh.htm
http://www.ucl.ac.uk/history/volterra/
http://members.aol.com/pilgrimjon/private/lex/rome.html

ABOUT THE DISTINCTION OF RIGHTS

Aberkane Hassen, *Contribution à l'étude de la distinction des droits de créance et des droits réels*, Paris, LGDJ, 1957

Aubry and Rau, *Cours de droit civil français*, Paris, volume 2

Baudry-Lacantinerie, *Précis de droit civil*, Paris, volume 1

Boiteux, *Commentaire sur le Code Napoléon*, Paris, 1852

Boquet Claude, *De l'opposabilité aux tiers comme caractéristique du droit réel: essai d'épistémologie juridique sur la base des droits allemand, français et suisse*; Genève, Avenir, 1978

Capitant Henri, *Introduction à l'étude du droit civil*, Paris, 1904

Catala (P), "La transformation du patrimoine dans le droit civil moderne", *Revue trimestrielle de droit civil*, 1966

Clavier Jean-Pierre, *Les catégories de la propriété intellectuelle à l'épreuve des créations génétiques*, Paris et Montréal, L'Harmattan, 1998

Dabin Jean, "Les droits intellectuels comme catégorie juridique" Paris, *Revue critique de législation et de jurisprudence*, 1939.

Delvincourt, *Cours de droit civil*, Paris, 1825

Demogue René, *Les notions fondamentales du droit privé, Essai critique pour servir d'introduction à l'étude des obligations*, Paris, Rousseau, 1911

Demolombe, *Cours de Code Napoléon*, Paris, 1854

Deruppé Jean, *La nature juridique du droit du preneur à bail et la distinction des droits réels et des droits de créance*, Paris, Dalloz, 1952

Duranton Alexandre, *Cours de droit français*, 2e édition, Paris, 1828

Ebke Werner F., Finkin Matthew W., *Introduction to German law*, The Hague, London, Boston, Kluwer Law International, 1996

Ginossar Samuel, *Droit réel, propriété et créance - élaboration d'un système rationnel des droits patrimoniaux*, Paris, LGDJ, 1960.

Josserand Louis, "Configuration du droit de propriété dans l'ordre juridique nouveau", Mélanges juridiques, dédiés à Monsieur le Professeur Sugiyama, Tokio 1940

Kruse Frederik Vinding, *The right of property*, London, New York, Toronto, Oxford University Press, 1939

Lesenne, *De la propriété avec ses démembrements*, Paris, 1858

Levis Marc, *L'opposabilité du droit réel*, Paris II, thesis, 1985.

Lois et Actes du Gouvernement, volume 1, Paris, Imprimerie Royale, 1834

Marcadé, *Explication du code civil*, Paris, 1886, volume II

Marty G. and Raynaud P., *Droit civil, Introduction générale à l'étude du droit*, Paris, Sirey, 1972

Michas H., *Le droit réel considéré comme une obligation passivement universelle*, Paris, thesis.1900

Mourlon and Demangeat, *Répétitions écrites sur le code civil*, Paris, 1896

Picard Edmond, *Le droit pur - Cours d'Encyclopédie du droit- les permanences juridiques abstraites*, Paris, Félix Alcan, 1899

Planiol Marcel, *Traité élémentaire de droit civil*, Paris, Pichon, 1908, and 1911

Pouillet Eugène, *Traité théorique et pratique de la propriété littéraire et artistique et du droit de représentation*, Paris, Marchal et Billard, 1908

Pothier, *Oeuvres*, Paris, 1847, IX, "Traité du droit de domaine de propriété"

Prodan C., *Essai d'une théorie générale des droits réels*, Paris, Thesis, 1909

Queru R., *Synthèse du droit réel et du droit personnel - Essai d'une critique historique et théorique du réalisme juridique*, Caen, Thesis, 1905

Rigaud Louis, *Le droit réel, histoire et théories, son origine institutionnelle*, Toulouse, thesis, 1912

Ripert Georges, *De l'exercice du droit de propriété dans ses rapports avec les propriétés voisines*, Aix, thesis, 1902

Roubier Paul, *Droits subjectifs et situations juridiques*, Paris, Dalloz, 1963

Terré François, *Introduction Générale au Droit*, Paris, Dalloz, 1998

Terré François, Simler Philippe, Lequette Yves, *Droit civil, les obligations*, Paris, Dalloz, 1999

Toullier Charles, *Le droit civil français*, Paris, 1830

Van Bemmelen, *Les notions fondamentales du droit civil*, Amsterdam, 1892

Villey Michel, "La notion romaine classique de Jus et le Dikaion d'Aristote", *La filosofia greca e il diritto romano*, Roma, Accademia Nazionale dei Lincei, 1976

Villey Michel, "Les origines de la notion de droit subjectif", *Archives de Philosophie du Droit*, Paris, Recueil SIREY, 1953-54, p. 163-187.

Voirin Pierre, *Droit civil*, Paris, L.G.D.J., 1999

ABOUT PATENT LAW AND INVENTORS' RIGHTS

Bertin (André), *L'ingénieur et les brevets d'invention*, Paris, édition du Tambourinaire, MCMLIII

Bonnet J., *Etude de la législation allemande sur les brevets d'invention*, Thesis Paris, 1902

Brunot Patrick, *La contrefaçon*, Paris, PUF Que sais-je? 1986

Calmels, *De la propriété et de la contrefaçon des oeuvres de l'intelligence*, Paris, Cosse, 1856

Casalonga Alain, *Traité technique et pratique des brevets d'invention*, volume 1, Paris LGDJ, 1949
Chavanne Albert, Burst Jean-Jacques, *Droit de la propriété industrielle*, Précis Dalloz, 1980

Lesoeur Marc, *Les droits de l'inventeur et le dépôt des brevets d'invention en droit interne*, Paris, Pedone, 1939

Lucas André, *La protection des créations industrielles abstraites*, Paris, Librairies techniques, 1975

Mousseron (JM), *Le droit du breveté d'invention, contribution à une analyse objective*, Paris, LGDJ, 1961

Munier (S.), *Les droits des auteurs de découvertes ou d'inventions scientifiques - Essai de philosophie et de technique juridiques suivi d'une proposition de loi*,Thesis, Nancy, 1925

Pouillet Eugène, *Traité théorique et pratique des brevets d'invention et de la contrefaçon*, Paris, Marchal et Billard, 1899

Roubier (Paul), *Le droit de la propriété industrielle*, Paris, Librairie du Recueil Sirey, 1952

Vivant (Michel), *Juge et loi du brevet*, Paris, coll. CEIPI, XX, Lictec, 1977

Wagret (JM), *Brevets d'invention et propriété industrielle*, Paris, Que Sais-Je n° 1143

NOTES

[1] Kohler, *Forschungen aus dem Patentrecht*, Manheinm, 1888, pp. 116 and following; *Handbuch des deutschen Patentrechts*, Mannheim, 1900, pp. 58 and following; see also Bonnet J. : *Etude de la législation allemande sur les brevets d'invention*, Thesis, Paris, 1902.

[2] Bonnet J., *op. cit.*, p.10.

[3] Bonnet J., *op. cit.*, p. 12.

[4] Bonnet J., *op. cit.*, p. 11.

[5] Bonnet J., *op. cit.*, p. 12.

[6] Bonnet J., *op. cit.*, p. 12. Translated from French: "...c'est sur l'idée, sur la conception que l'inventeur peut et doit exercer son droit... et non sur la forme périssable".

[7] Bonnet J., *op. cit.*, p. 13.

[8] Picard E., *Le droit pur - Cours d'Encyclopédie du droit-les permanences juridiques abstraites*, Paris, Félix Alcan, 1899.

[9] *Ibid.*, p. 118.

[10] *Ibid.*, p. 121.

[11] *Ibid.*, p. 120. Translated from French: "De chose matérielle à chose intellectuelle, les différences de nature et d'origine sont trop grandes pour que le même régime juridique puisse convenir."

[12] *Ibid.*, p. 109. Translated from French: "... les romains ne se rendirent pas compte qu'une chose purement intellectuelle pouvait être l'objet d'un droit cela répugnait à leur judiciaire éminemment positive et matérialiste".

[13] *Ibid.*, p. 104. Translated from French: "Il exprime l'action possible du premier [le sujet] sur le second [l'objet]; ce que le sujet est autorisé à faire de l'objet, comment il peut en user, jouir, disposer".

[14] *Ibid.*, p. 107.

[15] *Ibid.*, p. 107.

[16] Dabin Jean, "Les droits intellectuels comme catégorie juridique", *Revue critique de législation et de jurisprudence*, 1939.

[17] *Ibid.*, p. 413 n° 2.

[18] *Ibid.*, p. 438, n° 24.

[19] *Ibid.*, p. 433, n° 19.

[20] *Ibid.*, p. 434, n° 19.

[21] *Ibid.*, p. 434, n° 19.

[22] *Ibid.*, p. 434, n° 19.

[23] *Ibid.*, p. 437, n° 23.

[24] *Ibid.*, p. 438, n° 23.

[25] *Ibid.*, p. 446, n° 3. French text: "...les droit intellectuels sont des "droits sur les choses incorporelles" au sens strict du terme, [c'est-à-dire excluant les droits en général] marquant emprise sur ces choses, avec mode approprié d'usus, de fructus, d'abusus..."

[26] Roubier Paul, *Le droit de la propriété industrielle*, tome I, Librairie du Recueil Sirey, Paris, 1952, p. 103. Translated from French: "Le droit réel est celui qui donne la mainmise sur une *res*; le droit de créance est celui qui correspond à un certain crédit sur le débiteur".

[27] *Ibid*, p. 103.

[28] *Ibid.*, p. 104, n° 23.

[29] Translated from French: "Toute découverte ou nouvelle invention, dans tous les genres d'industrie, est la propriété de son auteur".

---

[30] Munier S., *Les droits des auteurs de découvertes ou d'inventions scientifiques - Essai de philosophie et de technique juridiques suivi d'une proposition de loi*, Thesis, Nancy, 1925.

[31] *Ibid.*, p. 253 / and Kohler, Urheberrecht an Schriftwerken und Verlagsrect; Klostermann, Das Geistige Ligentum.

[32] *Ibid.*, p. 260 Marquis De Vareilles-Sommières, "La définition et la notion juridique de propriété", *Rev. trim. dr. civ.*, 1905, p. 443-495.

[33] Munier, *op. cit.*, p. 262.

[34] *Ibid.*, p.262.

[35] Josserand Louis, "Configuration du droit de propriété dans l'ordre juridique nouveau", Mélanges juridiques, dédiés à Monsieur le Professeur Sugiyama, Tokio 1940, p. 95.

[36] *Ibid.*, p. 95-96.

[37] *Ibid.*, p 95-96.

[38] *Ibid.*, p. 95-97

[39] French text: ..."c'est une vue primaire que de vouloir confondre [les droits de propriété] avec leur objet... leur matérialité [des choses] laisse intacte l'immatérialité des rapports, des idées, des droits qui gravitent autour d'elles..."

[40] *Ibid.*, p. 98.

[41] *Ibid.*, p. 98 and p. 100.

[42] *Ibid.*, p. 101.

[43] *Ibid.*, p.101.

[44] Mousseron J.M., *Le droit du breveté d'invention, contribution à une analyse objective*, Paris, LGDJ, 1961; see also Mousseron J.M., *Traité des brevets d'invention*, *op. cit.*, p. 46 and following.

---

[45] *Traité des brevets d'invention, op. cit.,* p. 25 n° 22.

[46] Thesis, *op. cit.,* p. 17 p. 21-27 and p. 30 and Traité..., *op. cit.,* p. 8 and 9 n° 6.

[47] *Ibid.,* p. 105, 109, 185.

[48]*Ibid.,* p. 105. Translated from French: "Utile et rare, le résultat industriel nouveau présente les traits caractéristiques d'une valeur économique".

[49] *Ibid.,* p 146.

[50] *Ibid.,* p. 126.

[51] *Ibid.,* p. 129.

[52] *Ibid.,* p. 129 He quotes Chevallier J.: *De l'effet déclaratif des conventions et des contrats,* thesis,Toulouse, 1932, Dalloz, p. 17.

[53] *Ibid.,* p 130. Translated from French: "...est de réduire une entrave pratique ou juridique à l'exercice d'un droit antérieur".

[54] *Ibid.,* p. 137.

[55] *Ibid.,* p. 137.

[56] *Ibid.,* p 143.

[57] *Ibid.,* p 146.

[58] *Ibid.,* p.191 and following. Translated from French: "...un droit absolu portant directement sur l'invention définie à l'état de bien meuble incorporel".

[59] *Ibid.,* p. 267.

[60] In French: "maîtrise physique de la chose concrète préhensible".

[61] *Ibid.,* p 276, and Traité, *op. cit.,* p. 47.

[62] *Ibid.,* p. 276.

[63] Article 1 of March, 11, 1957 law: "The mere fact of the creation of a work of the mind confers on the author a right of incorporeal property exclusive and opposable to anyone".

[64] Vinding Kruse, *The Right of Property*, Oxford, Oxford University Press, Vol. I 1939, pp. 124-125, quoted in Ginossar, Droit réel, propriété et créance - élaboration d'un système rationnel des droits patrimoniaux, Paris, LGDJ, 1960, p. 2.

[65] See: Michas H., *Le droit réel considéré comme une obligation passivement universelle*, Thesis. Paris 1900; Rigaud L., *Le droit réel, histoire et théories, son origine institutionnelle*, thesis, Toulouse, 1912; Ginossar S., *Droit réel, propriété et créance - élaboration d'un système rationnel des droits patrimoniaux*, Paris, LGDJ, 1960.

[66] Capitant, "Introduction à l'étude du droit civil, 2d edition, 1904, pp. 76-78; Dabin J., "Les droits intellectuels comme catégorie juridique", *Revue critique de législation et de jurisprudence*, 1939; Marty G. and Raynaud P., *Droit civil, Introduction générale à l'étude du droit*, SIREY, 1972, p. 482, n° 302.

[67] Michas H., *Le droit réel considéré comme une obligation passivement universelle*, thesis, Paris 1900, p. 59.

[68] Translated from French: "le droit de jouir et disposer des choses de la manière la plus absolue, pourvu qu'on n'en fasse pas un usage prohibé par les lois ou par les règlements".

[69] Planiol M., *Traité élémentaire de droit civil*, book 1, LGDJ, Paris, 1908, 5th edition, n° 2159. Translated from French: "Tout droit est un rapport entre les personnes".

[70] *Ibid.*, n° 2159. Translated from French: "Un droit réel quelconque est donc un rapport juridique établi entre une personne comme sujet actif et toutes les autres comme sujets passifs."

[71] *Ibid.*, n° 2159. Translated from French: "L'obligation imposée à tous autres que le titulaire du droit est purement négative:elle consiste à s'abstenir de tout ce qui pourrait troubler la possession paisible que la loi veut assurer à ce dernier".

[72] *Ibid.*, n° 2160. Translated from French: "Ils diffèrent l'un de l'autre par deux caractères spécifiques, portant l'un sur le nombre des sujets passifs, l'autre sur l'objet de l'obligation."

[73] *Ibid.*, n° 2163.

[74] Demogue's works were no longer available and we worked on the basis of Rigaud's works quoting him, in *Le droit réel, histoire et théories, son origine institutionnelle*, thesis, Toulouse, 1912 p. 179.

[75] Compare with the solution of the enigma of the classification of rights, above. Translated from French: "Au fond il n'y a pas plus de droits absolus que de droits relatifs, car tout droit peut revêtir à la fois l'un et l'autre de ces deux caractères. Tout ce que l'on peut dire au point de vue scientifique, c'est qu'il y a des droits à contenu fort et des droits à contenu faible, des droits plus ou moins commodes dans leur exercice. Les droits sont tous des droits d'obligations, entre lesquels il y a des variétés, suivant les considérations pratiques"

[76] In Rigaud L., *Le droit réel, histoire et théories, son origine institutionnelle*, op. cit., p. 180. Translated from French: si "...le droit personnel est relatif de sa nature, en ce sens que le débiteur seul peut être tenu d'exécuter l'obligation, il est absolu en ce sens que les actes qui créent ou qui constatent le droit d'obligation existent à l'égard des tiers. Si le créancier n'est créancier que du débiteur, le fait qu'il est créancier existe *erga omnes*; de

même le débiteur, bien que ne devant qu'à son créancier, doit être tenu par quiconque comme étant débiteur"

[77]*Ibid.*, p. 196. Translated from French: "En réalité, il n'y a de division bipartite des droits que la suivante qui est toute de fait: les droits s'exerçant directement sur les choses et ceux qui se rapportent à un état de fait supposant l'existence d'autres êtres humains. Les droits sont tous des droits d'obligations, entre lesquels il y a des variétés suivant des considérations pratiques".

[78]See the references quoted in Ginossar S., *Droit réel, propriété et créance - élaboration d'un système rationnel des droits patrimoniaux*, Paris, LGDJ, 1960; p. 10.

[79] Bernard Jean, "Création scientifique et création artistique", *Revue des Sciences morales et politiques*, 1987, n° 4 p. 637. Translated from French: "L'imagination est le vrai terrain de germination scientifique"

[80] Revue des sciences morales et politiques, 1987 n° 3, p. 325 and following "De certains processus mentaux dans la découverte en mathématiques". Translated from French: "...qu'un des aspects essentiels de la découverte est la levée des inhibitions. L'inhibition vient de notre propre architecture [il s'agit de l'architecture mentale] que nous ne pouvons pas démolir".

[81] "Contraintes et libertés des modèles astrophysiques" *Revue des sciences morales et politiques*, 1987, p 555-556. Translated from French: "Quiconque touche à l'Univers touche au problème des origines, voire à celui de la création... " "... on croit trop facilement qu'on est quitte avec le réel pour peu que les équations soient correctes et les calculs exacts..".:"La mathématique est-elle le bon langage?... Ne sommes-nous pas prisonniers de Platon? Et de la beauté des mathématiques?".

[82] R*evue des sciences morales et politiques,*1987, n° 1 p. 7 and following; and p. 15. Translated from French: "On s'est aperçu, non sans surprise, que l'observateur (ou plutôt la méthode d'étude qu'il emploie) jouait un rôle si grand qu'il pouvait aller jusqu'à "changer" l'objet". "Ce n'est pas le monde réel que décrit la recherche scientifique, ce n'est que le résultat d'un dialogue entre l'observateur et le réel, un dialogue où l'observateur et ses méthodes sont aussi importants que le réel."

[83] Villey Michel, *La formation de la pensée juridique moderne, Cours d'histoire de la philosophie du droit,* Paris, Montchrestien, 1975, p. 17?

[84] *Revue des sciences morales et politiques,*1987, n° 3 p. 325. Translated from French: "Tout débute à un moment donné par la survenue d'une idée. Tout à coup, on se pose une question dont on n'a pas la réponse. C'est tout le contraire de ce que l'on fait en classe, en demandant aux élèves: "démontrez que ...".

[85] Jacob François, *Revue des sciences morales et politiques,* Science de jour, science de nuit", p. 59 and following. Translated from French: "La science de jour met en jeu des raisonnements qui s'articulent comme des engrenages, des résultats qui ont la force de la certitude..." "La science de nuit, au contraire erre à l'aveugle... Ce qui guide l'esprit alors, ce n'est pas la logique. C'est l'instinct, l'intuition".

[86] Hamburger Jean, "De l'art de raisonner en biologie et en médecine, *Revue des Sciences morales et politiques,* 1987, n° 1 p. 7 and following. Translated from French: "La biologie et la médecine n'ont pas seulement progressé par observations et outils nouveaux, elles ont progressé dans l'art de raisonner. Pendant des siècles, les chercheurs

furent tiraillés entre deux tentations opposées:l'arrogance subjective, qui croit pouvoir tirer la vérité de la seule imagination, et le réalisme passif, qui se borne à accumuler les faits observés et redoute toute cogitation. Peu à peu, il appparut que la méthode efficace exigeait un juste équilibre dans le dialogue entre les informations objectives et l'imagination du chercheur..."

[87] Pierre Daco, *Les prodigieuses victoires de la psychologie*, coll. Marabout n° MS 15, Verviers 1977, p. 239, 216,480. Translated from French: "une révélation qui surgit brusquement... L'intuition permet de connaître directement, sans raisonnement, et donne une conviction. Aucun jugement n'intervient. Certains tempéraments montrent une grande intuition naturelle"

[88] V.G. Jung, *Essai d'exploration de l'inconscient*, Coll. Folio Essais, n° 90, p. 61. Translated from French: "Beaucoup de philosophes, d'artistes et même de savants, doivent quelques unes de leurs meilleures idées à des inspirations soudaines provenant de l'inconscient."... "le mathématicien Poincaré et le chimiste Kékulé durent de leur propre aveu, d'importantes découvertes à de soudaines images révélatrices surgies de l'inconscient"

[89] *Ibid.*, p. 157. Translated from French: "Même la physique, la plus rigoureuse des sciences appliquées dépend à un point étonnant de l'intuition, qui agit par l'inconscient...".

[90] Brown Peter Lancaster, *L'astronomie, Observation de l'univers*, Paris, Edition des deux Coqs d'Or, 1986, p. 35.; see also aussi: Sagan Karl, *Cosmos*, éd. Mazarine 1981, p. 181.

[91] Jacob F, "Science de jour, science de nuit", *Revue des Sciences morales et politiques,* p. 59 and following

[92] Jung, *op. cit.*, p. 156. Translated from French: "... même un homme très intelligent peut s'égarer gravement par manque d'intuition, ou de sensibilité..."

[93] Michas H., le droit réel considéré comme une obligation passivement universelle, thesis Paris 1900, p. 31, p. 41: ..."les lois romaines avaient avant tout un but pratique, celui de régler matériellement les rapports des citoyens romains et des pérégrins entre eux. Pour les Romains, ... il est vrai de dire que le droit est engendré par les faits, et les besoins de la vie pratique ont toujours inspiré et comme imprégné les institutions juridiques de Rome".

[94] Michas H., le droit réel considéré comme une obligation passivement universelle, th. Paris 1900, p. 31, p. 41; Van Bemmelen, "les notions fondamentales du droit civil, Amsterdam, 1892, p. 222. Translated from French: "L'esprit de système n'était ni un de leurs mérites ni un de leurs défauts. Leur intuition juridique a toujours été fort supérieure à leur réflexion méthodique ".

[95] Villey Michel, *ibid.*, p. 276, p. 278. Translated from French: "... tout ce qui existe dans notre monde:c'est-à-dire, non pas seulement les objets physiques, matériels..., mais l'intégralité de l'homme, esprit autant que corps, et les institutions humaines et les institutions sociales".

[96] Villey Michel, "Le raisonnement juridique dans l'histoire", ARSP, arch. 1971, p. 47. Translated from French: "Je crois d'abord pouvoir poser qu'il est aujourd'hui établi chez les romanistes, que le discours des jurisconsultes romains n'est pas de type scientifique. La "science" (je prends le mot au sens ancien) était le discours de celui qui sait;qui dispose d'axiomes certains, de quelques vérités nécessaires, dont il est en mesure de tirer des conséquences nécessaires, de construire un

système déductif. Euclide, par exemple, opérait sur le mode scientifique. ... Que tel ne soit pas le discours juridique romain, je crois bien pouvoir affirmer que c'est un point unanimement reconnu par les spécialistes. Vous le trouverez souligné dans les grandes synthèses, particulièrement de Fritz Schulz et Max Kaser, sur la nature de la méthode juridique romaine".

[97] Aberkane H., "Contribution à l'étude de la distinction des droits de créance et des droits réels, Essai d'une théorie générale de l'obligation propter rem en droit positif français, th. Paris, 1957, p.10. Translated from French: "Selon que le pouvoir porte sur une chose ou qu'il est dirigé contre une personne, on dit qu'il s'agit d'un droit réel ou d'un droit personnel. Quoiqu'il en soit ces pouvoirs portent en définitive soit sur une chose, soit sur une personne, et l'on ne conçoit pas l'existence d'un autre élément sur lequel ils pourraient porter". L'auteur en tire la conclusion que "tous les droits doivent logiquement se ramener ... au droit réel et au droit personnel".

[98] That is to say a comprehensive power on a thing; see Villey, Le droit romain, Que sais-je? PUF p. 84.

[99] Villey, Le droit romain, Que sais-je? n° 195, PUF, 7th edition, p. 12.

[100] As we want to do nowadays when speaking about incorporeal property.

[101] Villey Michel, "Historique de la nature des choses", Arch. 1965, X, p. 272.

[102] *Ibid.*

[103] Michas H., le droit réel considéré comme une obligation passivement universelle, Thesis Paris 1900, p. 61. See also Villey, *Le droit romain*, Que sais-je? PUF, p. 44 about the contents of the Institutes.

[104] As everybody can access INPI's registers "stealing inventions" is therefore permitted.

[105] Picard E, *Le droit pur - Cours d'Encyclopédie du droit-les permanences juridiques abstraites*, Paris, Félix Alcan, 1899.

[106] Above, p. 8.

[107] Picard E., *op. cit.*, p. 123.

[108] *Ibid.*, p. 79. Translated from French: "un rapport de jouissance d'un sujet -sur un objet- protégé par la contrainte sociale"

[109] *Ibid.*, p. 129. Translated from French: "l'objet n'est pas en cause, mais uniquement le rapport, et c'est celui-ci qu'on fractionne".

[110] *Ibid.*, p. 130-131. Translated from French: "Il s'agit... d'une 'autorité' plus ou moins étendue pouvant s'exercer sur autrui, depuis la simple créance jusqu'à la puissance paternelle..."

[111] *Ibid.*, p. 129.

[112] *Ibid.*, p. 128-129.

[113] *Ibid.*, p. 128-129.

[114] *Ibid.*, p. 130; diagram p. 135.

[115] *Ibid.*, p. 132.

[116] *Ibid.*, p.135, see also his first part concerning energies.

[117] See diagram above p 44.

[118] *Ibid.*, p. 173.

[119] *Ibid.*, p. 107. Translated from French: "Sans cette contrainte agissant ou prête à agir, il est pur platonisme"

[120] Gaïus, Inst. II, 13-14.

[121] Kohler, in Bonnet J. *Etude de la législation allemande sur les brevets d'invention*, Thesis, Paris, 1902.

[122] Roubier, Le droit de la propriété industrielle, t I, Sirey, p. 102.

[123] Dabin J., "Les droit intellectuels comme catégorie juridique" Rev. crit. de Législ. et de jurisprudence, 445, n° 31. Translated from French: "objets les moins susceptibles de monopole".

[124] Terré and Weil, Droit civil, Précis Dalloz, 4th edition n° 244. Translated from French: "C'est le droit le plus complet que l'homme puisse exercer sur une chose"

[125] Aubry and Rau, Droit civil français, 2d book, libr. techn. 1961, p. 85; Terré and Weil, *op. cit.*, n° 243. Translated from French: "...un pouvoir direct et immédiat sur une chose".

[126] Terré and Weil, *op cit.*, p. 157.

[127] See Marty G. and Raynaud P., *Droit civil, Introduction générale à l'étude du droit*, Sirey, n° 143 à 146 and n° 301 à 308.

[128] Aubry and Rau, Droit civil français, book II, libr. techn. 1961, 7th ed. by Paul Esmein p. 85-86.

[129] Roubier P., Droits subjectifs et situations juridiques, Paris Dalloz, 1963, p. 340. Translated from French: "les droits réels.. ont été organisés... dans le cadre des biens du monde extérieur".

[130] Aubry and Rau, *Droit civil français*, 2d book, libr. techn. 1961, 7th edition, by Paul Esmein, p. 377; *comp.* Carbonnier J., *Flexible droit*, p. 243.

[131] Michelet J., *op. cit.*, p. 91 ss.

[132] Terré and Weil, op. cit., p. 268 n° 253.

[133] Roubier P., *Droits subjectifs et situations juridiques*, p. 344. Translated from French: "Notre droit civil est en principe établi sur la base des biens corporels ou matériels".

[134] *Ibid.*, p. 345. Translated from French: "le droit moderne, grâce à la théorie des *res incorporales*, va plus

loin, qu'il assimile aux biens les autres droits comme les droits de créance, les droits de clientèle (fonds de commerce, brevets etc...) et l'auteur admet la possibilité de droits réels sur tous ces droits..."

[135] Térré and Weil, *op. cit.*, p. 268, n° 253; aubry and Rau, *Droit civil français*, Book II, libr. techn. 1961, p. 13, note 12. Translated from French: "L'expression 'biens' ... désigne les droits à caractère économique, les droits patrimoniaux. On a cependant l'habitude de distinguer les biens corporels, qui sont les choses matérielles, en tant qu'elles sont susceptibles de droits et les biens incorporels, qui sont les droits, droits réels, personnels, ou intellectuels"

[136] Marty and Raynaud, *op. cit.*, p. 476 n° 296.

[137] See Mousseron J.M., *le droit du breveté d'invention*, *passim*. On the distinction of goods, see Arch. *Les biens et les choses*, 1979, book 24.

[138] Adda Didier, "Contrats informatiques, la clause de réserve de propriété"; *Zéro Un informatique,* 27 February 1989.

[139] Catala P., "La transformation du patrimoine dans le droit civil moderne", Rev. trim. dr. civ., 1966, p. 201. Translated from French: "Longtemps, cette notion de propriété sans 'corpus' parut choquante aux interprètes rompus à la théorie romaine des droits réels. L'essence de la propriété n'est-elle pas la chose corporelle, objet du droit? Mais des études récentes ont montré que le droit de propriété vaut surtout par l'opposabilité absolue de la protection dont jouit son titulaire".

[140] Josserand, "Configuration du droit de propriété dans l'ordre juridique nouveau", Mélanges juridiques, dédiés à Monsieur le Professeur Sugiyama, Tokio, 1940.

[141] *Ibid.,* p. 96; compare with: Villey, "Les origines de la notion de droit subjectif", arch. 1953-54.

[142] Josserand, *op. cit.,* p. 98. Translated from French: "Immatériel et ainsi idéalisé, le droit de propriété va pouvoir porter sur des biens incorporels et non pas seulement sur des choses...." "...il exerce son emprise sur son objet sans s'identifier à lui".

[143] *Ibid.,* p. 101. Translated from French: "Devenue moins matérielle la propriété en est devenue plus fragile".

[144] Source: Industrial Property, October 1979, laws and treaties, p 006.

[145] Houssard G., report Palewski J.P., AFPPI, annexe 1 quoted in Mousseron, thesis, *op. cit.,* p. 258. Translated from French: L'Etat est évidemment souverain, et puisque c'est lui qui concède le brevet, il a toujours la faculté... de supprimer ce privilège ou de n'accorder à l'inventeur qu'une récompense ou une rémunération équitable".

[146] *Ibid.,* p. 173. p. 36.

[147] Isore, *De l'existence des brevets d'invention en droit français avant 1791,* Revue d'histoire du droit, 1937.96, quoted in Vivant Juge et loi du brevet, *op. cit.,* p. 6. Translated from French: "Que sont donc nos brevets modernes, sinon des privilèges concédés dans un but d'intérêt social?"

[148] Cass., req., 25 July 1887, R.S; 1888 1.1. Translated from French: "Attendu que les droits d'auteur et le monopole qu'ils confèrent sont désignés à tort, soit dans le langage usuel, soit dans le langage juridique, sous le nom de propriété;que, loin de constituer une propriété comme celle que le Code civil a définie et organisée pour les biens meubles et immeubles, ils donnent seulement à ceux

qui en sont investis le privilège exclusif d'une exploitation temporaire...".

[149] Cour de Limoges, 22 December 1936, Ann. 1938, p. 64. Translated from French: "La délivrance d'un brevet apparaît comme un acte de gouvernement de la part de la puissance publique, quelque chose comme un acte de souveraineté".

[150] Quoted in Casalonga, p. 39.

[151] Tribunal Civil de la Seine, 11 August 1836, Translated from French: "Si le prétendu inventeur au lieu d'une découverte nouvelle ne donne à la société qu'une découverte déjà consignée et décrite dans des ouvrages imprimés et publiés... le prétendu inventeur est alors déchu de son brevet... "

[152] Quoted in Lesoeur Marc, Les droits de l'inventeur et le dépôt des brevets d'invention en droit interne, thesis, 1939, p. 27. Translated from French: "des privilèges exclusifs d'une exploitation temporaire".

[153] Vivant quoting Aristotle La politique IX and 11 stressed that monoply comes from "monos" and polein" meaning selling alone.

[154] Concerning the concept of "good", see: Archives de Philosophie du Droit, *Les biens et les choses*, Paris, Sirey 1979, n° 24.

[155] Compare with: Terré: "L'évolution du droit de propriété depuis le Code civil", *op. cit.*, p. 9.

[156] Catala P., "La transformation du patrimoine dans le droit civil moderne", *op, cit.,* p 198, n° 18.

[157] Roubier, *Droits subjectifs et situations juridiques, op. cit.*, p. 347-348.

[158] Calmels E., *De la propriété et de la contrefaçon des oeuvres de l'intelligence*, Paris, Cosse, 1856, p. 4-5.

[159] M. Vivant, Juge et loi du brevet, coll. CEIPI, XX, Lictec, 1977, n° 4, p. 2.

[160] See Roubier, Le droit de la propriété industrielle, book 1, Sirey, Paris, 1952 p. 64.

[161] *Ibid.*, p. 65.

[162] *Ibid.*, p. 92, n° 21.

[163] Moniteur, 24 March 1841, quoted in Calmels E., *op. cit.*, p. 48. Translated from French: "Le droit des auteurs n'est pas une propriété, c'est une parole obligeante du législateur; ce n'est pas une définition légale".

[164] French text: "N'entend l'Assemblée Nationale porter aucune atteinte aux privilèges exclusifs ci-devant accordés pour inventions et découvertes, ..., lesquels auront leur plein et entier effet..."

[165] French text: "L'Assemblée Nationale, considérant que toute idée nouvelle, dont la manifestation ou le développement peut devenir utile à la société, appartient primitivement à celui qui l'a conçue, et que ce serait attaquer les droits de l'homme dans leur essence, que de ne pas regarder une découverte industrielle comme la propriété de son auteur."

[166] Translated from French: "idées nouvelles dont la manifestation ou le développement peut devenir utile à la société".

[167] Translated from French: "L'assemblée nationale, considérant que toute idée nouvelle, dont la manifestation ou le développement peut devenir utile à la société, appartient primitivement à celui qui l'a conçue, et que ce serait attaquer les droits de l'homme dans leur essence, que ne pas pas regarder une découverte industrielle comme la propriété de son auteur.

Considérant, en même temps, combien le défaut d'une déclaration positive et authentique de cette vérité peut avoir contribué jusqu'à présent à décourager l'industrie française, en occasionnant l'émigration de plusieurs artistes distingués, et en faisant passer à l'étranger un grand nombre d'inventions nouvelles, dont cet Empire aurait dû tirer les premiers avantages ...".

[168] Translated from French: "Quiconque apportera le premier, en France, une découverte étrangère, jouira des mêmes avantages que s'il en était l'inventeur".

[169] Translated from French: "Tout moyen d'ajouter à quelque fabrication que ce puisse être un nouveau genre de perfection, sera regardé comme une invention".

[170] Law 98-620 of November 8, 1984 Semiconductor Chip Protection Act, la Propriété Industrielle March 1985.

[171] Law n° 87-890 of November 4, 1987 on the Protection of topographies of Semiconductor Products and on the Organization of the National Institute of Industrial property OJ, 5 November 1987; JCP 1987, II 60781; see also at a European level: the Council Directive of December 16, 1986 on the legal protection of topographies of semiconductor products (OJ EEC January1, 1987 L 1987, N° L24/36).

Other books by Anna Mancini, Ph. D:

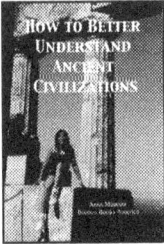

HOW TO BETTER

UNDERSTAND

ANCIENT CIVILIZATIONS

MAAT REVEALED,

Philosophy of Justice in Ancient Egypt,

by Anna Mancini Ph. D

COPYRIGHT LAW IS OBSOLETE

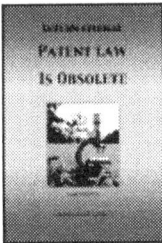

INTERNATIONAL PATENT LAW

IS OBSOLETE